What Others are Saying

"In this technological age, Facebook has become a useful networking tool. In Jen Carle's new book, she explores all aspects of the Facebook experience . . . Jen's stories are real and honest, spiced with her unique and entertaining humor. A year's worth of her Facebook adventures makes a fun read."

—Esther LoPresto,
author of *Where's My Other Sock?*

"[Carle] uses charming humor and personal reminiscences to illuminate on what life is like when you are suddenly thrust into reengagement with everyone you have ever known. The encounters are at turns funny, titillating, fulfilling, and wasteful."

—Jack Gilden,
former political columnist
The Baltimore Jewish Times

"This book is a lovely portrait of one woman's discovery of Facebook and how social networking changed her life. Through finding, friending, and connecting in ways like never before, the author reframes our thoughts about social networking."

—Joshua Miller
Owner of Zenawood Entertainment, movie director, and author of *The Heart of Love*

My College Boyfriend Dumped Me for You

My College Boyfriend Dumped Me for You

Can I Add You as a Friend?

Jennifer A. Carle

Tate Publishing & *Enterprises*

My College Boyfriend Dumped Me For You

Published by Tate Publishing & Enterprises, LLC
127 E. Trade Center Terrace | Mustang, Oklahoma 73064 USA
1.888.361.9473 | www.tatepublishing.com

Tate Publishing is committed to excellence in the publishing industry. The company reflects the philosophy established by the founders, based on Psalm 68:11,
"The Lord gave the word and great was the company of those who published it."

Cover design by Rebekah Garibay
Interior design by Jeff Fisher

Published in the United States of America

ISBN: 978-1-61739-360-0
1. Biography & Autobiography, Personal Memoirs
2. Family & Relationships, Interpersonal Relations
10.11.02

Dedication

While I was writing this book, both of the title characters stopped contact with me. The college boyfriend, realizing he had a real life, dropped off of Facebook altogether. The girl he dumped me for unfriended me. I guess I shouldn't have been surprised. Perhaps she couldn't keep up with my witty repartee.

Because of being unfriended by the boyfriend stealer, I would like to dedicate this book to all the people who have been unfriended on Facebook and know it. You are all better without them.

Author's Note

I joined Facebook in January 2009, and by February of 2009, I knew I needed to write a book about this social network. I was reconnecting with people that I hadn't seen or spoken with for decades. In their own right, my Facebook friends are truly special and amazing people to me, and it doesn't seem to matter that I've known some of them for a week or went to high school with them.

When I decided to write my book, I of course had to post my big announcement as my wall status. My friends were thrilled and all wanted a copy. I also let everyone know that if they did not want to be a part of this book to let me know. I also mentioned that I did not name names unless I was writing about my husband and children.

I did hear from a few Facebook friends that did not want to have their anecdotes written in my story. I also asked a couple of friends from college if I could write about them because their lives seemed so different from our long ago days of sitting on the concrete wall next to the fire lane of Washington College, smoking cigarettes with our white sunglasses and big, overly treated hair.

A couple of relationships changed during the time it took to write this book. Once close, say anything friends became distant. I'm not sure why the dynamics changed, but they did, so I strongly felt the need to send private messages to these "friends" and let them know that they were in my book and if they wanted to be removed to let me know. I did not hear back from them, so I kept their interactions with me because I thought these people added so much to the chapters. I truly hope that they will be as honored to be portrayed in these pages as I was to write about them.

My Introduction to Facebook

I was coming back from New York on a sold-out train. My seatmate and I struck up a conversation to pass the time. She was a seventeen-year-old high school senior who was going to see history being made in Washington, D.C. I was checking my e-mails to pass the time when I saw that I had a message from a friend of mine with whom I used to work. He wrote that I should join Facebook and add him to my friends list. I laughed out loud and asked my seatmate if she thought people my age and older were too old for Facebook. My son was on Facebook often, catching up with his friends from camp. My seatmate was elusive at first but then kindly told me that Facebook was really good for her generation. Yikes. Where was my AARP card?

I e-mailed my friend and asked how he could possibly find the time for Facebook. Like most retirees, he was busier than when he worked forty-hour weeks. My friend told me that Facebook was the easiest way for him to stay in contact with his friends and business associates *because* he was so busy. I wasn't sure about being a part of a social network. I was a social person on some level. When I did my book signings, I gravitated toward the spotlight. I had to, or else I wouldn't sell any of my books. I was social at work because I was the first face and impression a patient had when they walked into the office. Keeping to myself or acting withdrawn was not going to cut it in my work as an office administrator. So I wavered between feeling social enough already and peer pressure. If my friend who had a life was on Facebook, shouldn't I be as well? As my train pulled into Penn Station in Baltimore, I decided I would check out Facebook. It wouldn't hurt to look, would it?

I came home and hopped on the computer (after greeting my family). I explained that I received an e-mail from a friend about joining Facebook. Since my husband knew this friend, Ken was fine with me trying a new computer interest. My older son was polite about my quest. I was crashing his social network party, and we both knew it. We made an instant pinkie swear that we would not become friends with each other. Since my son was on the other computer already, he gamely assisted me on my Facebook quest. I joined Facebook and wrote for my status, "Jen is thinking she is too old and too computer illiterate to be on Facebook." Instantly there were two comments to my statement. My cousin in Florida answered that there was no way I was too old, *and* she sent me a hug. The second comment came from a good friend whose house I can see from my bedroom window but whom I hadn't spoken with in too many months. She said that if she could get the hang of Facebook anybody could.

At 7:00 p.m. on Monday, January 19, 2009, I began my Facebook experience.

Looking For Friends

My son patiently and respectfully showed me how to navigate Facebook. It started with my writing a profile about myself. Since I was one of my favorite topics of conversation, I was blown away by my sudden shyncss. "What should I say?" I asked my son.

"Anything you want, Mom."

The questions on the profile were fairly straightforward. I had to answer what I was looking for on Facebook. *Uh… nothing?* It then gave me choices, like was I looking for friendship, networking, or love? I answered "friends" and "networking." That seemed safe. I went on to write about my favorite bands, books, movies, activities, and quotes. I answered questions about my educational background. I wrote where I went to high school and college and the year I graduated, and then the fun began!

Facebook showed me some people I might know and might have wanted to be friends with based on my educational background. "Now what?" I asked my son.

"Look at the people and see if you want to be friends with them." *Oh.*

I saw a picture of a girl I went to high school with. I didn't have any contact or relationships with the girls I went to school with as soon as I stepped off the stage with my diploma in my hand. I usually threw the alumni newsletter in the trash because, quite frankly, high school was not the happiest time for me, and I wanted to be rid of the memories. One day I actually read the newsletter, and the girl whose picture was before me was a topic. I remembered it to be a fascinating story, and I felt my frozen insecurities beginning to thaw. *What? She had a bad day too?*

I sent her a message saying that I read the article and that I had been thinking of her off and on. She added me as her friend and went on to describe some of the details of that article.

"I have a friend," I said to my son.

"Good, Mom."

I was instantly transported to my third-grade playground. I wasn't the last one chosen for dodgeball. I had a friend.

The friend I e-mailed on the train didn't have me as his friend. I e-mailed him, *How can we be friends?* He replied that he would look for me in the pages of Facebook and add me to his friends list. Get out! I had two friends.

I saw a picture of a boy I went to college with. I had actually interacted with him on several occasions in my adult life, so I sent him a message. Around midnight I thought I should get off of Facebook and go to bed.

The next morning there were five messages on my phone from people that had either accepted my friend request or initiated having a friendship with them. *Oh my gosh! Look at that!* I showed my son. He replied for me to have fun with it.

My husband, Ken, had no idea what was going on. As far as he knew, I already had friends. Why look on the Internet to make a friend? "Honey," I said, "you have got to get on Facebook!" There was really no way to describe what I was doing that didn't sound a little . . . uh . . . desperate and pathetic. "Just join!"

I turned on my computer at work and went to the Internet. I did have work-related things online, so logging on was legitimate. After I did my work-related items, I went on Facebook. I saw a picture of a guy I knew (sort of) in college who had asked me to be his friend. We were going back twenty years, and I just wasn't sure he was whom I thought he was. He looked much different in his picture than he had in college. So we wrote back and forth. Our conversation had nothing to do with college. We chatted in present tense about our families, jobs, and interests. We had a similar mind-set, which I found to be refreshing and made conversing relaxed and not filled with awkward small talk.

He told me a little about his job. He didn't love what he was doing and had different ambitions for himself, but his job did pay the bills and allowed him to share a nice lifestyle with his family. I told him that I loved my job working for my husband, but I never saw myself as a glorified secretary. I explained that once I began using behavior modification in my daily functions, I felt like I was really using my college education. He made a comment about me being one of the few who actually learned enough in college to apply it twenty some years later. I laughed out loud when I read that. He had a wicked sense of humor that paralleled my own. Although I couldn't place him clearly from college, I knew that as adults we'd easily share a repartee that could be friend-worthy. We both ended our chat to go back to work, but I looked forward to our next conversation. I hadn't learned how to initiate a conversation, so I hoped my friend would want to get in touch with me again.

After that one morning on Facebook, I was hooked, and I bagged doing real work.

I Don't Think You Know Me Now, But...

I began connecting with a lot of people from college. I loved college and knew it would be fun to find out what everyone was up to now that we were "established." I didn't ever seem to make it to any of the reunions, so for me this was a reunion on the computer. People had posted pictures of their children, pets, and/or significant others and had written some comments about them. That was really fun to see and read. These people had children my kids' ages. We went to the same vacation spots. We had similar interests. I was fascinated. It was easy for me to picture a beer bottle in the hand of college mates. I found I recognized everyone better that way. Now I was getting to know them again.

The way Facebook worked was you had your friends, and then you got to see who your friends were friends with. That was fun. Of course, we had all gotten older and had gone on with our lives, so most of these people I didn't know. When someone I knew was mentioned as a mutual friend by the Facebook gurus, I asked them to be my friend. Third-grade-on-the-playground thoughts made me nervous that these people may not have wanted to be my friend. *What then?*

I came home from work, briefly interacted with my family, threw something together that passed for dinner, and got back on Facebook. Did they respond? Did I have friends? They did, and I did! My son came in and checked his Facebook account. "Alex," I asked, "what happens if someone doesn't want to be my friend? Will Facebook say that I'm just a big, fat loser?" Because he was a teenager, he had a knack for texting his friends, listening to his iPod, and talking to me while on Facebook simultaneously, so I considered him a reliable source for all things electronic.

"No. You'll never know," he responded.

"I don't get it." Alex explained that if I chose someone as a friend that didn't want to be my friend, I just wouldn't hear from them. There would not be a message saying that so-and-so did not want to be my friend. I sighed. "Thank goodness."

So I continued to look around. I felt like a stalker. I was inviting myself into other people's conversations, and no one cared. Facebook was not like a chat room where the discussion group knows that you are "eavesdropping." I decided to pop into a conversation my cousin was having. She was family, so I felt comfortable butting into her world. She was telling one of her friends about her plans to go to the beach that upcoming weekend. My cousin lived in Florida, and she was a real lover of sun, saltwater, and sand. I commented on her beach plans by asking if she got to go to the beach very often. My cousin responded that she didn't get to go as often as she wished, so when she did go, she made a full day of it. I told her to have a great time, and she said she would post pictures. I had no idea what she was talking about.

I had a good friend in college who lived two rooms down from me. She was a girly-girl. Her room always smelled like hot mulled cider, although I never was offered or saw any. She painted her door a soft mauve and had framed pictures on her walls. That was a far cry from the Monet posters I had taped to the walls in my room, which smelled like bunny poop because I had a bunny that always figured out how to get out of her cage and into my sweaters and underneath the bed and pooped anywhere she chose. She had graduated a year before me but was on campus quite a bit. She often invited me and some other girls over to her house a couple of towns away for dinner. We kept in touch for the first couple of years after I graduated. We stopped corresponding for no real reason other than being busy, but we caught up again a few years later when she and I were both bridesmaids for a mutual friend. We lost contact again for about fifteen years.

On Facebook, she responded that she was very glad to hear from me but that she would e-mail me so we could have a private conversation. *Huh?* I thought we could just write in each other's inboxes, not that I knew how to do that yet. I thought back to my earlier postings. I could definitely be snarky. It was a blessing and a curse. *Nope,* I thought. *I did not post anything even remotely catty, gossipy, or mean. I was being my kind and polite self.* I waited for a couple of days for an e-mail from her. I didn't get one and never heard from her again after that initial correspondence. According to the Facebook wizards, we have continued to be friends.

Not Friends?

I decided to look for my best friend from college. We had lost touch several years ago. I had asked my college's alumni representative if there was a current phone number and/or e-mail address for my long-lost friend. The alumni department had both. I wanted to let her know that I had written a book about my dog. She would have remembered my dog Winn very well. Winn attacked her dog over a rawhide chewy. We had to squirt Winn with water from the hose until she backed off. I did not get a response to my e-mails, so I left a message on the machine of the number I was given. My telephone message said the same thing as my e-mails. I had written a book; she and her husband were referred to in it, and I wanted to mail her a copy and needed her address.

I never heard anything from her. I called the alumni department and asked if she was still alive, and she was. *Oh good,* I had thought at the time. *She's not dead; she just hates me.* I remembered a phone conversation I had had with her several years prior. I remember sitting outside on my front stoop, drinking a glass (surely not my first) of wine. I was a drunkorexic at the time and used my wine calories as something to sustain me. Drinking my calories was a fun trick my eating-disordered mind played. I needed no food, just wine. The gist of our conversation was that I was bummed we never got to see each other anymore. She had family in Baltimore, and on the eastern shore. Surely we could have met up somewhere. She was busy, busy, busy with life. I said something snarky along the lines of, "Well, if I were driving in your state, I'd come see you." She replied that my family and I would be more than welcome to visit anytime. If she gave me her address, I was too far gone with wine and hurt to remember. We never spoke again.

Maybe I could find her on Facebook. I wasn't sure how to go about looking. There were so many different ways to find people, and I only knew of two, searching for her with the old e-mail address I had for her or going through the people from college who graduated when we did and were on Facebook.

I found her. I found her! I ran and told Alex and Ken that I found my friend. She was okay and definitely not dead, just as the alumni department had said the year before. Alex got it, but Ken still didn't get Facebook. He was just happy because I was, and he liked my friend and her husband. He hoped we could all get together with our boys.

I was stuck and asked Alex what I should do next. He told me to request her as a friend and look at her profile. I did both. I noticed that we had no friends in common, which I thought was odd because the girly-girl from our dorm was also in her wedding. My college friend had one friend. I looked up her profile to see if there was anything special written. There wasn't. I looked in her "notes" section. That was the area of Facebook where you wrote down certain things, either on your own or in response to someone else's request. She had notes. They were private.

I left her alone and went on to find other people to be friends with, as well as trying to figure out how to send stickers, hugs, candy, and other applications to my existing friends. I figured out how to send my husband candy hearts and attach a little message to go with it in his inbox.

I contacted my other cousin and told her to join Facebook. Like me, she had reservations because Facebook was her daughter's department and she dared not intrude. I told her that Alex and I were not friends. I didn't want to know what he was talking to his friends about, particularly the adorable girl from camp who, anytime she saw Alex, would say, "Let me give you a hug." Good for him, not for me. Alex and I had sworn not to be friends, although Alex did agree to be friends with Ken. That made sense. They liked doing manly things together, so being each other's Facebook friend would probably not be the intrusion that having Mom as a friend would be. My cousin signed up.

Facebook was catching on quickly. Although Facebook celebrated its fifth birthday in the early part of 2009, a lot of my contemporaries were just hopping on the bandwagon. The "older" Facebook friends had only been on for six months at the most. They were the ones who easily navigated the site and all its options. As for me, I just did a lot of cutting and pasting from my e-mail.

Stumbling Down Memory Lane

I got to thinking about the friends of my friends. There was one guy from college who was really, really nice and funny, and he had a lot of different friends. He was a big, loveable goof who made our crew practices at five in the morning almost bearable with his off-the-cuff comments. He was the person who made me do a double take, wondering if I really heard what he had just said. I posted on various people's wall that if they knew where he was on Facebook, I'd like to be his friend. Most people wrote back that they hadn't seen him or heard from him since college. One of my friends, the one who asked me to be his friend and then initiated our lunchtime discussions while we were supposed to be working, said he saw my missing friend at a party two years before. He mentioned the name of his friend who had the party, and the lightbulb went on! I remembered who he was! So, since our postings back and forth had been very friendly, I was vulnerable and opened up some to him. "Was the friend who had the party the same one who was best friends with a boy I dated?" I asked. I added that I thought we had dated during our sophomore year, although I wasn't positive. He replied that yes, I had dated that person my sophomore year. Oh no! I had to think! I felt like posting a big apology on my profile to him and everyone else I went to college with who was now a friend of mine on Facebook, saying something along the lines of, "I don't know what I did or said, but I get a gnawing feeling in the pit of my stomach when I see you here on Facebook, so I'm sorry. I'm not that bratty, stuck-up, mean girl in real life."

So I asked if he was one of those boys who sang, "Watch it wiggle, see it jiggle..." from the old Jell-O commercial when I ran across the quad one time. He wisely said that he wasn't a part of that. Not having anything else to say, we actually went back to our real jobs.

The next day my Facebook friend posted that he had been in touch with his friend whom I used to date. According to my Facebook friend, my boyfriend from sophomore year did not recall being cruel enough to sing that song about me. I confirmed that it was absolutely true. Who could make that up? I said that I had mentioned the incident in one of my books but I did not name names. I wrote that I honestly didn't think the "Jell-O jingle guy" and I were mature enough to have the deep relationship we had. I didn't go as far as apologizing for being, essentially, me. I did, however, feel some regrets that I had conveniently sequestered in one of the filing cabinets in my brain for twenty years. My friend wrote that we all had regrets about college. That was really nice of him to say, and I felt the gnawing in my stomach die down.

I had remembered the good things about college, mostly when I was a senior. I had had a tight group of friends, I had been in a committed relationship with a very handsome lacrosse player, and, most importantly at that time, I was thin, super thin. I blocked out my first couple of years in college when I acted like the privileged prep-school graduate who was smarter and better than anyone else.

There was the time my freshman year when I went to a dance with Jell-O jingle guy. After the dance was a party. I stood up Jell-O guy and went to the party with a boy I'd had a crush on since orientation. Jell-O guy was understandably ticked off and went to his friends' rooms, got extremely drunk, and began screaming about what a witch I was. I was sure I had just given him a look that meant "So what?" or "Whatever," along with the necessary eye-roll.

Ah, my college life had come back to me. I was fascinated by Facebook, and canceling my membership because of one guy that I behaved badly toward was not an option. I decided to stay busy, not by working or parenting, but by joining Facebook clubs and causes. The Maryland SPCA was listed as a cause, so I joined. I also added SPCA friends as my friends, such as the trainer who had seen the potential in Winn those many years before and had a sharp-tongued sense of humor that I had forgotten about until Facebook.

Facebook Messages

When I checked my phone each morning, I found more and more messages from Facebook than I did work-related topics. Ken was mocking me and my need to see if I had any friends on Facebook. Thankfully, we were so very secure in our relationship that he knew I was doing nothing more than seeing if anyone had responded to my friend request. I was sending Ken stickers and candy and little love notes. I hadn't abandoned him for my new, old friends. Ken never remembered to check his inbox to see the collection of items I had sent him.

One of my original four Facebook friends had a really impressive and eclectic group of friends. He was a Baltimore guy and super nice. Although our lives intermingled on our home turf, I didn't really get to know him until college. He was a lacrosse player and in the fraternity that counted almost the entire lacrosse team as members. Unlike his fraternity brothers, my friend had excellent manners, respected women, and ate his food with utensils. He was out of place and perfectly in place, and I really admired that about him. Because of his strong sense of self, he was friends with *everyone.* Whenever Facebook recommended a new friend, he was almost always the mutual friend. Jokingly I asked if he could introduce me to a couple of Baltimore Ravens football players. Sadly, his connections did not go that far.

One of the people mentioned as a mutual friend was my "real" college boyfriend, the one I had dated my junior and senior years, the one who wouldn't wait while I put our relationship on hold so I could write my thesis. Memories came flooding back. Twenty years later, I envisioned myself being this unreasonable, snobby girlfriend who put a lot of unnecessary pressure on our relationship. I was so caught up in me: my weight, my thesis, my life after college, my caloric intake, and my questions of "Does this dress make my butt look big?" He had gotten on with his life.

We had remained friends for a couple years after he graduated. He called me to tell me he was getting married to a girl who did not go to our college but whom I had seen and spoken with on campus. She was so pretty and nice and the one thing I never thought I could be: relaxed. She clearly enjoyed him for who he was at that given moment. She was not mentally foreseeing disasters with him as I had. She loved him completely. He loved her. It was so obvious by his voice. I don't think I ever heard that sort of emotion in his throat before. So that was that. I sent them a gift and hoped for a lifetime of happiness for them. I kicked myself for letting that one get away. Jeez Louise. Was I a stupid-head or what?

I wrote to him and asked if we could be friends. Our exchange was friendly and relaxed and *normal.* I wasn't hanging on every word he spoke or ignoring him completely like in college. In a few short minutes of chatting on Facebook, we caught up on twenty years. It was that easy. No drama, just enjoying catching up and bragging about our kids. I was reminded that we were friends in college before our relationship changed to a committed status. I felt relieved that I was no longer that spoiled brat from college who thought she was better than everyone else. The real me, the one who was thoughtful and kind and helped kittens and puppies and had a really quirky outlook on life, was confident enough as an adult to just be me without trying to impress anyone. The real me was looking forward to reconnecting with my old boyfriend, who had become a professional family man. The real me was not a shameless flirt trying to impress him somehow.

Friendship Confirmed

I was trying to process my new Facebook life. My son started Facebooking with his friends from camp and school. They were his current friends. I was reliving college. I was cringing and smiling at the same time. I got a message that someone had confirmed me as a friend.

I had broadened my horizons. I had my college friends, but I also had SPCA friends, neighborhood friends, and the friends that were the members of the clubs I had joined. One club was called "If you're OCD and you know it, wash your hands!" I really enjoyed that group, and I knew that the members would appreciate my need to vacuum and clean the sparkling kitchen countertops several times a day. I wasn't hurting anyone; I was just being quirky me.

I almost fell off my chair when I opened the message and read that my best friend from college, the one whom I'd been searching for off and on for years, confirmed me as a friend. *Oh my gosh!* She wrote a note saying that it was good to hear from me. She was not one of those people to spend a lot of time on the computer, so she was just getting started. I envied her constraint. I was on the computer fairly often before Facebook. I was hooked now. I was thinking of seeing if there was a twelve-step group for Facebook, but I decided I didn't want to admit my problem yet. I wanted to have more fun.

On her profile, she posted pictures of her son and vacation spots that they enjoyed. I reached out and touched the photo of her son who was just three months old the last time I had seen him. He looked just like his mom and dad. It was really neat to see good genes at work. She also posted on her profile that she no longer was teaching and was enjoying her time at home ferrying her son to all of his events. Her note continued that she also wished me luck on my sort-of career as an author. I wanted to write back and let her know that without her there would not have been any books. I would not have adopted my dog from the Maryland SPCA if my relationship with my significant other at the time had been like her relationship. I wanted what she had for myself. If I hadn't realized that, there would be no vicious dog to adopt. I'd be stuck in a relationship that was safe but not really enjoyable.

I didn't write anything and let her have the last word. I really hoped that she would send me another message and let me know what she had been up to for the last fourteen years. I didn't want to seem desperate to catch up with her. I noticed she accepted many other people as friends. I knew that we would reconnect at some point on those Facebook pages.

You Tried To Get My Boyfriend to Dump Me. Can We Be Friends?

As I continued to join new clubs, update my profile, and catch up with my cousin in Florida, the recommendation of friends I might have known continued to appear from one of my original four friends. Other than the Baltimore Ravens, who didn't he know? A photo of a pretty woman with her child came up. I didn't know who she was. Like me, she had joined Facebook with her married name. I wrote to my friend. *Was this person really the person whose name I had known her by twenty years ago?* He wrote back, "Yep."

I sat and thought. I wrote to him, "Was she always pretty?"

He responded, "Yep, and tall."

I wrote one more time and said that I remembered who she was but that I felt so threatened by her in college. I didn't realize how pretty she was. He had no answer. So I thought it over. As I remembered, she had had a huge crush on my old boyfriend and tried to weasel her way into his life any chance she could. My rational adult brain said that it probably didn't happen that way. Our relationship was slowly slipping away, and she took advantage of an opportunity. I tuned into my rational mind and thought about becoming friends with this girl.

I thought about being friends with her while driving. I considered it at the grocery store. I really wanted to ask someone, but whom? My husband? My son? They did not need to know what a drama queen I was in my past life. My friend was staying out of it. I really felt like writing to him and asking if she was nice. I reverted back to my third-grader-on-playground self and realized I wanted to know if she and I could be friends. Would she like me?

Oh boy, did I need a reality check! Who cared? If she didn't want to be friends, she'd ignore the request. Did I want to be her friend *because* she had tried to steal my boyfriend and I wanted to be the mature one? How dumb would that be? She lived twelve hundred miles away in a cold, snowy part of the country. I was never going to see her again.

I sent her a note asking if she remembered me. I was my rational self, not the self who subconsciously wanted to say, "I was the one whose boyfriend you wanted all for yourself." I knew it didn't really happen that way, but because I was done with him, I didn't want anyone else to like him. Again, I cringed when thinking of my former self.

Being Invited to Join Groups

One day I looked on my Facebook page, and there was a request for me to join a group. Was this a joke? Was this a virus? I asked my son. "Can you tell by the name if it is a group you recognize? If you know it, it's probably not a virus." What a good kid. I did know the name of the group.

On my old college campus, a fire lane went from one heavily traveled road to another, less traveled road that paralleled it. Everything happened on the fire lane. All the latest news and gossip was reported from the fire lane. The group I was invited to join was about life in college from the fire lane. Oh my!

The memories continued to flood into my brain and, consequentially, the pit of my stomach. *The fire lane*... This was not just an ordinary fire lane. This was where it all happened on campus. From the fire lane, we could watch who was hooking up with whom, who was wearing in the morning the same clothes they had worn the night before. Adjacent to the fire lane were the "hilltop" dorms. They had, at one time, all been fraternity houses. The fraternity of rowers for the crew team had a couch they pulled out so we could watch or be watched in comfort.

I opened the page and joined the group. A girl from college, with whom I'd become friends after we'd both worked a summer at the same beach before junior year, had scanned pictures of us alumni friends and posted it onto the group page. I was so impressed that she had kept the photos in the first place.

How did she know where these pictures were? I would have thrown them away in my need to be tidy. I was tagged in a photo. That meant there was a picture of me that was sent to my wall. It was my favorite picture of my college best friend and me, the one who had so recently connected with me on Facebook. I remembered the photo so vividly, but I wasn't sure if someone had given me a copy or had just shown it to me. We were sitting on a brick wall near the student union, laughing. I had a wavy hair permanent and wore light pink sunglasses. That was amazing! All the girls had big hair and white sunglasses. That was the style in the 1980s. It was so funny looking back at the way we were.

I wrote on the wall of the girl who had posted the pictures, "Do you have a picture of me sitting in the fire lane, facing the couch, where my hair was in a French braid and I was wearing a light-colored tank top?" It was my favorite picture of me individually because I was thin and relaxed-looking. I remembered liking my arms and the fact that I only had one chin in that photo. She asked if it was a yearbook picture. I wrote that I wasn't in the yearbook my senior year because all of the photographs taken of me were with my old boyfriend, and we had broken up before the yearbook was published. She said she'd look.

How Did You Know That?

The person whom I'd befriended that was friends with the Jell-O guy wrote that he forgot whom I had dated until he read my wall-to-wall with my friend who had scanned all the pictures. We were both on Facebook at work and were engaging in a private chat.

"How did you read that post that was on someone else's wall?"

"Easy," he responded. "I'm friends with her too. I can read what is written between my Facebook friends if there is a mutual connection."

Think. I had to think! What had I written that was revealing about myself or my relationship with others? I scrolled down to previous posts. What had I said that was incriminating? Nothing. My heart was racing.

"I didn't mean to offend you," my friend chatted to me.

"Oh no, of course you didn't offend me. I was just trying to figure out this whole Facebook network thing." Thank goodness we were writing back and forth and he was not able to see my deer-in-the-headlights look I got when I was thinking on my feet.

I found out that chats between online friends and conversations posted to an individual's inbox were private. Anything else that was written on the pages of Facebook was for anyone to read. Why had my one friend who got me started on this whole adventure read a wall-to-wall conversation I was having with someone who was not his friend? He was a voyeur. He read my side of the conversation, and it was interesting enough for him to follow the thread of the story. I was stunned. Not that my friend was a voyeur—to each his own—but because he read other people's conversations. Why would anyone do that?

The answer was as obvious as my Facebook name—because we could. Facebook had such a network of friends of friends that anyone could read snippets of others' threads as long as there was just one mutual friend to link it. If a comment sounded funny that a friend's friend made, I opened up the section and followed the thread. It was just like eavesdropping on a phone call, except it was better, because we all knew that someone would read about someone they didn't care about. Well, I didn't know then, but I knew now. Again, I felt that cringing feeling in my stomach. I had written a book about myself, so I wasn't shy about saying things about me. What had I said about other people? Was I snarky? I prayed I hadn't been.

Requests

When I would go onto my Facebook page, there was an icon on the bottom right corner that listed notifications. These notifications were updates that told who responded to which person's pieces of information they had posted on Facebook. At the top right, there was a box that indicated if there was a friend or group request. I loved that. I was third-grader-on-the-playground again as I opened my requests. Some of the requests were disappointing. I was not a fan of the requests to send my friends things like stickers or drinks or accessories. I did send beads to all my friends on Mardi Gras and a couple other things here and there, but not to the extent that some of my other friends did. They sent stuff like crazy. I began to ignore requests to accept shoes, handbags, flowers, martinis, and the dreaded stickers. I was able to decide if I wanted to accept or ignore people's requests. I was so sick of stickers and lipstick! I promptly hit the "ignore" button. Then I panicked. Did I just hurt someone's feelings and do so in a public forum? Should I send a note saying that I didn't mean to offend, I was just not in need of another item? Could I delete my "ignore" choice and just accept the "Live to Shop" sticker?

I practiced. My Florida cousin was great about sending me things. The idea was for me to accept the item and send some of my own to others. I pushed the "ignore" button. I figured if there was a problem I would hear about it from her sisters. I didn't. I didn't read any notes from my cousin because she didn't write on my wall or make a comment as to my current status. Was this the Facebook version of the silent treatment? I didn't like it. The third-grader-on-the-playground in me got chosen last for dodgeball.

A couple of days later, there was an update that she changed her relationship status from "In a Relationship" to "Single." She wasn't giving me the silent treatment; she was off of Facebook for a while. If I had thought about it, I could have looked up her activity to see if she had been writing to everyone but me. Phew! It wasn't me and the fact that I was ignoring my cousin's gifts. It was my cousin trying to get her life together.

I was requested to join different groups. A couple of groups were about the Maryland SPCA, so I joined them. Others were political or religious. I had no problem voting or praying, but I did have a problem making my affiliations public. I put enough of myself out on Facebook that was quirky. I didn't want to start anything controversial or argumentative. The "Ignore" button got increasingly easier to choose.

Quizzes

I noticed that some of my friends were taking quizzes and then posting their answers on their profile. Some of the quizzes looked really fun, so I tried to figure out how to answer the questions myself. One quiz, "25 Random Things About Me," was extremely popular, both on Facebook and with mainstream culture. Radio DJs would ask callers for random facts and tell the caller to pretend they were filling out the Facebook quiz of random things. I was all about random. I loved the randomness of random.

One of the original four friends was asked to take the "25 Random Things…" quiz by a relative of his. He wrote on Facebook that he didn't think anyone would care. I responded that the random things were probably boring to him, but to his friends from college who hadn't seen him in twenty-odd years, his random facts would be fascinating. I even mentioned something random about me to give him a boost.

So he filled out his twenty-five and attached my name to the results. I didn't know what that meant other than I could read what he wrote. My friend had written some things that were poignant, funny, sweet, and profound. I liked the adult version of him even more than I had the college version. By attaching my name, or tagging me, my friend wanted me to copy the quiz and answer on my own. So that's how it worked... You couldn't take certain quizzes unless someone attached your name to it. So I listed my twenty-five, and I sent my request for others to fill out the questionnaire. Other people weren't as quick to respond as I was. I would write to my friends, "So how's your twenty-five coming along?" More friends than I would have liked responded that they were too busy for silly quizzes. How could that be? They weren't too busy to convince me to participate in Facebook antics; why were they suddenly too busy?

I guess my responses to the random things were worth reading because I was sent all sorts of questions to fill out. There were the quizzes asking about what I liked. There were topics about everything under the sun. Like the gracious recipient I was, I answered within a day and forwarded the request to however many of my friends Facebook required. The first several quizzes were fun. Then they got boring. Also, I was busy at work and couldn't find the time to answer the questions. I noticed that most of my requests for friends to give their own answers were ignored.

I went to a friend's inbox and wrote, "Why do you not answer any of the questions I send to you? I'm sad." He wrote back that he really enjoyed reading my answers but he wasn't the type of person to put his life out for the world to read. Why was he even on Facebook? There had to be enough innocuous random for the more private people to use.

Thank goodness my responses were good. I tried to keep everything light and airy. One random thing I wrote was that I sometimes thought I was a terrible mother and wife. The rest were breezy. No sense in scaring my friends away.

The quizzes got out of control. They were being sent two and three times a day. One of my original four friends did something brilliant. He was forwarded some questions and answered them but then did not send them to anyone. His responses were on his wall for all to read, and if anyone wanted to answer those questions, they could just click on the quiz name and pull it up. Thank you so much!

Heart Be Quiet; Head Start Talking

I was really enjoying making new friends on Facebook. By the beginning of February, I had thirty-eight of them. I was pretty impressed with myself because I didn't have that many friends in real life. I was amazed at the number of friends some people had. They had hundreds. What kind of friendships were these? Would these people all be invited to their wedding? My thirty-eight were not "wedding friends." In fact, I only consistently corresponded with my original four and maybe three others. The remaining thirty-one friends were interesting enough to warrant my keeping occasional tabs on them to see what was going on in their lives.

The sad fact was I liked Facebook way too much. I would keep it on my computer when I wasn't doing work. I read other people's walls; I waited for something to be written on mine. It was like waiting for water to boil. Sadly, it took about two weeks of this to realize that having Facebook on my screen all the time was really boring. It was much better if I checked in periodically to see the updates. Unfortunately, I didn't have enough of a life outside of Facebook to warrant just an occasional glance, and I forced myself to do something else whenever I had the urge to stare at Facebook. My thirty-eight friends were not staring at the computer waiting for the latest update on Facebook. I felt fairly certain that if they were, those people would not be my friends.

A friend of mine from long ago wrote on his wall very infrequently. When he did, it was about something fairly spectacular, like taking his wife skydiving. In my opinion, it was worth the wait. Many of us wrote about wearing mismatched socks and that a coworker ate the friend's lunch: dumb, innocuous stuff. One day the skydiving friend sent me a message asking me how he could get my books. Ah, great question. I responded with where all my book signings were to be held in the upcoming weeks. Since he was out of the state, he didn't seem interested in driving for hours to buy a one-hundred page paperback. So I mentioned the usual suspects that were online. He asked if they were already signed. They weren't. I didn't get this "autographed by the author" status. I really couldn't think who would have cared that my name was scribbled on the inside. All of my signed books were personal and addressed to the reader. My books about my dog Winn were usually signed for the dog of the house. So I mentioned about getting his address and mailing them and figuring out what shipping and handling would cost. I secretly hoped he would make a drive over for one of my signings.

My Facebook friends were very encouraging about my signings. "I can't wait to see you and pick up a copy," one wrote. Another said, "We're going out of town. So sorry to miss this one. See you next time?" Others confirmed the time and location. My book signings, which were always a lot of fun, became Facebook friend reunions. There was a lot of hugging and chatting and introductions of family members. I loved it! I was selling books, seeing friends live for the first time in a decade or so, and they got to watch me be the same quirky, funny person they remembered. Adding an author title to my somewhat short list of accomplishments hadn't changed me at all.

My husband, Ken, and I went away for the weekend, and when I came back home, I hopped on Facebook. My skydiving friend was on Facebook too. I asked in his inbox if his weekend was good. A bunch of new pictures had just been posted from college in the 1980s, and I admitted that some of the memories from college made me "want to throw up in my mouth a little." He responded with something about time healing old wounds and memories. We all had regrets from college. My own list of regrets from freshman and sophomore years alone would have filled volumes. I always tried to end my correspondence with him first so I didn't look like I had nothing else to do besides be on Facebook. I had work piling up around me on my desk. I was getting notices from organizations asking if I had received their requests for information. I had. I'd get to it as soon as I had a free moment.

My skydiving friend and I had several more snippets of conversations over the course of a few weeks. I had mentioned that I had given up all sugar and white flour for Lent. I was stunned that other people were giving up Facebook for forty days. Were they serious? How could they give up Facebook? To me, that was like saying they were going to give up breathing until Easter: impossible.

I was fine for the first couple of weeks, and then I started to get really cranky. The woman at the deli counter of our local specialty market told me my order wasn't ready because I was too early to pick it up. A word to the wise would have been to never accuse a person with strict punctuality rules of being too late or too early. The other would have been to not say anything less than kind to anyone who had not had cookies, cakes, candy, or pretzels and crackers for sixteen days. I thought fleetingly about jumping over the counter and pinning her down with my watch in her face. Fortunately, the person who had taken my order went and got it for me out of the refrigerator in the back. Imagine that! There was more than one Jen in the Baltimore metropolitan region!

So I wrote the very condensed version of my sandwich story to my skydiving friend, and he wrote back that I was just as funny as he remembered and that he was glad we all turned out okay. That comment did something to my heart. I was happily married to the best person *ever* with two children and a budding writing hobby. I tried to live life each day being the best person I could be, and I was always thankful to God each night before I went to sleep. So I happened to mention my silly little heart-flutter to God. *Please forgive me for spending too much time on Facebook,* I prayed. *Please don't let me be distracted from the things and people that really matter. Also, God, would you mind giving me back my adult heart and taking back the skipping teenage one?* Jeez Louise! My life could be complicated enough at times without Facebook.

Very shortly after that, two things happened: my husband, thanks to his being on Facebook, met his former high school sweetheart for dinner downtown, and my skydiving friend got off of Facebook, never to be seen again. My sons asked me if I was jealous about Ken going out to dinner with his old girlfriend. I honestly said that I was not. They were two people who met a long time ago and over three hundred miles away from Baltimore. This was a chance meeting that only could have happened with Facebook. Ken and his friend had fun catching up, as he told me that night. They split the check and the cab fare. The two of them had reminisced about the old days and caught up on the present tense. My husband did not appear to be giddy or overly excited about his dinner out. He just said that it was great catching up with her after all the years. Ken was no different in his thoughts and feelings for me, and his actions proved to me that old relationships were just that: old. What attracted us to people in school or college didn't necessarily attract us to them now. I got rid of my fluttery heart from college and kept my fluttery heart that my husband gave me.

So as I was about to fall asleep, I said, *Thank you, God, for giving me my grown-up heart back. Now I am in sync with my brain. I will not spend as much time on Facebook now. You've shown me the way back to what is important.*

Stress is Much Better When Shared With Friends

For spring break in March, Ken took the boys down to Florida for their annual migration to visit the grandparents. I stayed at home for my annual keeping-the-house-clean happy dance. The day after they left, I got a call from our local hospital. I did not think anything of it since I knew the director of the foundation for that hospital and had just recently used my new book as a sponsor for the upcoming golf challenge. It was my coworker's husband calling to inform me that my coworker was very sick and in the hospital. She was going to have to stay for a few days while they ran tests.

I was very sad and worried for her, but I knew the hospital she was in was one of the best in the area. Since the office was closed for ten days, she would be able to recuperate at home and not worry about missing time at work. My coworker did get better, and she was discharged from the hospital. She called me and asked if she could work part time until she got her strength back. Her doctor told her to be off work for three weeks, but my coworker was getting agitated from doing nothing at home and thinking about the work that was piling up on her desk.

I eagerly agreed. The first few days we were back at work after an extended leave meant never-ending phone calls, faxes in piles, mail to sort through, and general organized chaos all around. Having my coworker back would allow me to get work done since we would both be answering the phone. So the first day our office reopened, she came in for a couple of hours in the late morning.

She didn't look well, but she had been pretty sick. The next day she came in for almost a full day. I was a nervous wreck and kept asking if she wanted to go home. On our third day back, I was in the parking lot looking in my purse for my card-key to enter the building. I dug around in my purse for a good ten minutes. I thought that I should have just walked around to the front of the building and used the automated doors.

I got to my desk, and my husband came out of the room where he had been consulting with a patient and said that my coworker was really sick. She was waiting for me to come into the office so she could go to the hospital. I felt guilty for spending so much time looking for my card-key. She could have been at the hospital ten minutes sooner. So she left, and she didn't come back for a little over two weeks.

My husband's medical office was an anomaly compared to the other settings in the area. My coworker and I did the jobs of three people, and Ken did his job as well as ordering his supplies. When we answered the telephone, the patients heard our voices, not a machine with verbal and numerical prompts. In a world that was becoming increasingly robotic and sterile, we were one of the few places that offered a friendly greeting over the phone. We knew most of our patients' voices before they introduced themselves and competently listened to their questions and wrote down notes for Ken. Because we had all been working together for six years, some of the basic, non-medical questions we could answer for the patient and ease their concern. Every once in a while, if we were both on the telephone and the third line rang, our automated system would answer and let the patient know we would be right with them or that they could leave a message. If the patient left a message, I would retrieve it as soon as I hung up from my previous call.

When my coworker left, I didn't want the stress of her workload to cause her to get even sicker, so I called our medical program office and asked them how to do my coworker's job and enter the numbers properly in the computer. I was extremely slow doing her job. What would have taken her an hour or two to input took me a whole day. That meant that my job wasn't getting done.

I went onto Facebook. I wrote, "Missing: one brain. No reward will be given if found, as it is overused and not working very well." Oh my gosh, I was stressed. I could practically feel my heart jumping out of my body. The Prozac I took for my anxiety wasn't working. I couldn't even think about how I'd have felt if I hadn't been taking many, many milligrams of the magic medicine.

I stopped concentrating on learning my coworker's job and used the last hour of my day to do my work. There were a few things that could wait for a day or two before completion, but there were little things that had to be done each afternoon to ensure a smoothly running next work day. My sons did not get picked up from school until after five o'clock. On Fridays I urged them to find a play date or sleepover they could get themselves invited to. My guilt-o-meter was on overload, but there was nothing I could have done at the time. I was already coming into work on the weekends.

A friend of mine responded to my status, "So it is safe to assume a reward will be given if you do not get your brain back?" This guy was a friend from college. He had been very laid-back at school and extremely popular because he was so easy to get along with. He had such a brilliant sense of humor on Facebook, which I didn't remember from college. I had asked him once why he didn't answer any of the quizzes that were sent his way, and he had answered by sending me a link to Jack Hardy quotes. I opened up the link as I was sipping my coffee that morning and spit it into my screen as I read the first quote! I responded that I had a mess to clean up and needed to get off Facebook. When I read this "brain" response, I once again laughed, water this time, out of my mouth and onto the screen. I wrote that I was beginning to think that every time he wrote something I would spit my drink out in laughter.

I felt so much better! The work was going to have to wait. I needed to play with my kids and dog. I was writing on Facebook to a friend whose son and mine went to the same school. I explained that sometimes the basic text-speak for laughter wasn't enough. There were occasions where *lol* (laughing out loud) wasn't enough of a laugh. *Rotfl* (Rolling on the floor laughing) was visually funny and usually the correct response. She and I were chatting back and forth when she said that her son had laughed so hard his swallow of milk came out his nose. I cracked up! I responded that it was still okay to do that when a kid's eleven years old. I confessed, "I still do that sometimes!" That was it! I wrote, "Do you suppose if I created 'laughing water out my nose' (*lwomn*) it would catch on?" She said that she would definitely use it since she got a hilarious and gross mental image of me laughing water out my nose.

My workload at the office was overwhelming. I would walk in and look at my desk and immediately have trouble breathing. I plugged along, slowly and just barely competently, doing some of my coworker's job as well as my own. The telephone was making me insane. I couldn't get to it before the automated system did because I was working with numbers and did not want to lose my place to answer the phone. Normally, if someone left a message, I would have listened to it right away. While my coworker was out, I let the machine take ten messages before stopping what I was doing to retrieve them. I turned the phone to "do not disturb" so I could see the line light up when it was ringing but would not hear it. Ken flipped out. "You have to answer the phone," he said. I told him I was going to answer the phone; I just didn't want to hear it. He didn't understand that, so I turned the phone sound back on and began to get crushed with every ring that resonated. Ken came back to my desk and asked why I wasn't answering the phone. I couldn't respond because I was on a different line.

We did have caller ID, which we installed because sometimes our patients would get confused and not remember their phone number in order for the doctor to give them a call back. Caller ID allowed us to make sure we knew the name and telephone number of all of our patients whose names came onto the screen. One patient called and left a message, saying he would call back. I rolled my eyes to myself. He called and I answered. He asked his question, I answered it, and we hung up. He called back. He had forgotten to tell me something. I took the message and told him I would call him back if I had a problem finding the answer to his question. If I did not call him back, that meant everything was fine and the doctor would call him later on. The patient called again. "I hadn't heard from your office," he reasoned. "I didn't want there to be a problem I didn't know about." I did not mean to be snarky. I really did mean to be nice and tolerant and professional. I told him, in a fairly curt tone of voice, that everything was fine. That's why I *hadn't* called him. He was just checking. I was just losing it.

I wrote on my Facebook page, "I am trying to channel my fear of the unknown and my nervous energy into something positive." My friend who made me spit twice wrote back that he could only imagine what I was going through. That was so nice! I got a pat on the back and a buddy hug from my Facebook friend. It didn't make my stress go away, but it made me feel like someone was out there if I needed to blow off steam.

Yes, That Was Me with the Jeep

When I was in high school, I went to a very elite all-girls school where, once she turned sixteen, the girl got a car and the obligatory trip to Europe. The girls got Volvos, Saabs, Mercedes, BMWs, and other, well . . . European cars. One girl got a Porsche. It sounded like it had a lawn mower engine inside it, but she had managed to fly over the campus speed bumps and take out every bunny or squirrel that happened to have been in her path. As for myself, I got grounded. On my sixteenth birthday, I got to hear the "immature and irresponsible" lecture for the millionth time.

I lived thirty-six miles away from school. I carpooled with four other girls, which made the driving easier for our parents. My mother quickly realized that by not letting me drive, she would have to do it for the rest of her life. I had no immediate plans for becoming "mature and responsible." She was furious with me and herself. I didn't deserve a car, and she didn't want to drive me and the other spoiled brat girls who whined that they had asked their parents for a ski holiday and had only gotten a trip to the Caribbean.

She looked to her husband for guidance. She got none, but I did get a car... sort of. My mother and her husband brought home for me, as my very own car, a postal Jeep. It was painted magenta and had the steering wheel on the right-hand side. There were two benches that ran parallel to the sides of it and a tray in the front left side where another seat would have gone. I guessed the tray was for holding the mail. I had to be very careful getting in and out of the Jeep because it was top heavy and would easily tip over if someone leaned on it. Also, my passengers had to be evenly seated, preferably by weight, so it would not tip over. When I got inside and slid the door shut, I could see the gravel in our driveway. There was a gap between the body of the car and the door.

I didn't know what to say. "Thanks? Are you insane? Do you really just hate me that much?" The Jeep was made by a company that also made four-wheel drive vehicles and farm equipment. My mother reasoned that my Jeep would be solid and sturdy and that I would feel safe in it (as long as the weight was evenly distributed and no one leaned on it). I wondered how I was going to pull this thing off. I hated being in the spotlight. I dressed, talked, walked, and smoked just like everyone else. I was anonymous in school. I very rarely spoke up even when I knew the answer. I hated calling attention to myself. Now I had a Jeep, a *magenta-colored* postal Jeep with the steering wheel on the right-hand side and metal benches for seats.

Every girl's school had one, only one. The European cars were a much more popular choice for the girls. The other students with the one, lone postal Jeep in school were much different than I. They were athletic, outgoing, smart, funny, pretty, confident, popular, and on and on. I was plain-looking with braces and greasy hair that had no bounce or style. I thought I was stupid, and I guess I became that way. I had no friends really. A couple of girls would hang out with me, but I got the feeling that they were doing so because there was nobody else. Essentially, I felt I was the *anti*-postal Jeep personality. The interesting part of having a bizarre vehicle like a magenta postal Jeep was no one wanted it. The kamikaze classmate who ran over bunnies with her Porsche found that she was without a car almost every time she went to retrieve it. Our campus backed up to a busy four-lane road, and her car got stolen many times.

So I managed to get through my last two years of school and even had my senior picture taken next to my Jeep. The Jeep easily carried all of my things that I would need for my freshman year in college. Since it had no real seats, the inside of it was a big vacant box with plenty of storage space. As long as everything was packed and weighted down evenly so I wouldn't tip over, I had no trouble driving the ninety miles from my mother's husband's house to Washington College on Maryland's eastern shore.

The interesting thing about Washington College, and all colleges, I supposed, was the demographics of the students. Some came from private schools. Some were on scholarships. Some students even lived in Chestertown and walked to campus for their classes. They were the "townies," a bunch of, in my mind, poor, uneducated, small-town kids that probably didn't know a Corona from a Budweiser, much less how to correctly pronounce Sophocles or wear the right designer clothes. I was such a snob, a snob in a magenta Jeep. I was my own oxymoron.

The Jeep was as popular as I had become my freshman year. Someone very quickly figured out that it was perfect for transporting kegs of beer from the liquor store to the dorm. The Jeep became "The Kegmobile." Everyone loved that they could all pile in and drink beer as long as their weight was evenly distributed. The Jeep embraced the late bloomer in me. In high school it made me stand out and feel even more insecure. In college the Jeep combined my two freshman favorites: beer and popularity. The summer before my junior year, my Jeep died a very slow, painful, pitiful death on Route Forty as bolt after bolt fell into the road. The bolt that held the engine in place fell to the ground of the service station I had been wise enough to pull into. I went back to college with a nondescript red Ford Escort and never thought of the Jeep again.

When I was chatting down memory lane with the first friend from college on Facebook, I had asked him a question randomly. I figured that since I didn't really remember him from college he didn't really remember me. He wrote that he remembered my red Jeep. Oh no! He knew who I was for sure! I was that snobby, bratty girl from private school who was dating his friend and who had a serious drinking issue. I didn't dare correct the color. I wanted to slip under my work station. *He knows,* I thought.

He knows I was the one who got alcohol poisoning in his dorm before Christmas break and passed out in the trash can. "I thought that was you," he wrote back.

I could not think of anything this friend had done that was memorable in college. He hung out with two guys who were so over-the-top that they managed to suck all the air out of any room they entered. Apparently they maintained that friendship for over twenty years. So even though I couldn't remember anything embarrassing about him in college, it was obvious that he was comfortable enough with who he was not to have to draw any attention to himself. In an instant, I thought of the girl who went to college, drank way too much, got put on academic probation, and was popular. I felt that familiar twinge of regret I got as an adult looking into my college life. I hated that stupid, magenta Jeep, but then I came back to my senses and realized it wasn't the Jeep. I had made really poor choices and did some incredibly naïve things my freshman year in college, and I happened to have a magenta Jeep that was top heavy.

Making the Most of Facebook

When someone wrote on Facebook, they were able to add a link or pictures or music to whatever they had posted. I was extremely envious of those people. I was never sure my comments were published at all; adding something was out of the question.

I had become friends with the mothers of our sons' football team. We had had so much fun yelling and cheering and watching our boys go at it against other schools. While our boys didn't always win, the moms and I were sure to entertain with our catcalls and enthusiasm. Alex had a classmate that looked very similar to him. I found that I cheered for that boy as often as I did Alex. I commented once in sixth grade flag football that Alex sure was getting a lot of playing time. The other boy's mother spoke up and told me that I was not watching Alex but her own son. That cracked me up! My parents did the same thing. "Look at Alex go!" they would cheer. "Clearly the coaches really like him!" I would point to Alex on the sideline and mention that it was the other boy playing. My mother often told me I was wrong. She knew what her grandson looked like. The other mother just laughed and said nothing.

I really missed the closeness of the football parents. My son had opted out of winter sports to participate in the school play, and in the spring he played tennis. Most of his football buddies played lacrosse. Fortunately, Facebook was the answer to my post-football letdown.

One evening, the mom who had the son that looked so much like mine posted pictures with her status that her house was for sale. The pictures were beautiful. The house was amazing. Who would move from there? I commented on her pictures by asking why in the world she would move. She wrote back that because of circumstances that were out of her hands she needed to sell the house and move somewhere else. I didn't know how to respond. She and I were not close friends, but we enjoyed each other's company at the football games. We had a mutual friend, one of my original four, who was really good at turning the worst situation into something laughable. I was hoping she could help put a positive spin on that disaster.

A few days later, I offered to help her pack her things or help her in any other way. I loved packing. It was the whole process of wrapping things, finding a way for them to fit in the box, and making it safely from one location to the next. I hated getting my hands dirty, and having newspaper print on my hands was extremely difficult for me to deal with, but packing had a lot of advantages that made dirty hands almost tolerable. Every couple of days or so, I asked how she was doing and reminded her that anytime she needed help to let me know.

In early March 2009, Facebook changed. It was very confusing for me to figure out who could see which posts. In fact, for a while, I was the only one who could not see my own comments. I got a message from a friend saying that she had received the pictures I had sent to someone else. I too was getting information not addressed to me. I had to change my password. How irritating was that? Facebook changed completely, and *I* had to change my password to be a part of this nonsense? I seriously considered quitting Facebook at that moment. I walked away from the computer and did not visit Facebook for several days. I missed my friends, though, and decided to change my password and get back on.

My husband and sons were getting ready to go to Florida for spring break. I wrote on Facebook that the time could not move quickly enough for me to drive them to the airport. I was going to be *free* for ninety-six hours. (Not that I was counting or anything.) My friend that was moving was also on Facebook and wrote me a private chat message. The message made no sense at all, and I thought that thanks to the new and unimproved Facebook I was receiving someone else's conversation.

She had asked if I were going away for spring break and had read my comment about packing up the guys. She wrote for me to have fun. Was she kidding? I was already mentally doing the happy dance. My friend mentioned that she wished she was going to Florida but she was sending her son instead. In the little world of Facebook, it became apparent that she and I were the only two people in "private school land" not going to Florida for spring break. "We should definitely get together," I wrote. We would be the only two pasty, pale people on campus and would need to stick together. "And it's free," she responded. True. We would stick together with our pale skin and not have to pay for the privilege of looking that way.

"So do you want to?" she chatted on. Of course I wanted to be pale with her. I got the feeling she had never been pale on spring break before. It was no big deal. I would definitely stick by her. Poor thing. "What are you talking about?" *Me?* I was talking about sticking by her side on campus for the rest of the year so we could be pale together. "So do you want to come to the book signing?"

Ah yes. Facebook was freaking out again. In its weak attempt to be fresh and up-to-date, conversations were being lost by the users. My friend restated her whole conversation about how a famous author was coming to the school where she worked to talk about her latest book. The lecture was free. Was I interested in attending? Oh. I had missed everything she wrote. I would love to go to the event. I liked other people's book signings as much as my own. I was thrilled that she asked me.

She also took me up on my offer to pack. She had found a new house, and the settlement date was only three weeks after the day she signed the contract. I attended the lecture at her school and, a week later, started to help her pack. I really got to know her well. I was loving my face-to-face experiences with my Facebook friends. She and I were total opposites in a lot of ways. She held on to things, and every bowl, napkin ring, or cheese spreader had a story. I held on to nothing. I hated clutter. I didn't like holding on to things because it might be valuable someday. Where had my grandparents come up with that? My motto was along the lines of "use it or lose it," or "when in doubt, throw it out."

There were special items that had been in her family for generations. I was not to touch those. She didn't let herself touch them either. Her parents were going to take care of the priceless family heirlooms. She chatted. I packed. She packed. I washed my hands. We both drank several Diet Cokes infused with what they called vitamins but what we found out later was caffeine. She and family members were going to move all the boxes and small, lightweight furniture. A moving company was hired primarily to take the baby grand piano and anything else that fit. We chatted, packed, and drank Diet Coke for hours. Periodically, I'd ask her if the box was too heavy to lift. She would lift it and declare it fine for moving. I went home feeling enriched from the friendship I had sealed.

Asking Facebook Friends for Help

I was never good at asking for help. I was great at offering it, though. My friend who made me spit on my screen was taking a survey. He threw out a random question and asked his friends to weigh in. Should he get a vasectomy, or should his wife take birth control pills? Oh boy, did I have a lot to say. I could have offered opinions on just about any topic. "Do *not* make your wife take the pill. She is a woman nearing forty. As she ages her hormones will be out of whack anyway, and the pill will not be helpful. Have you not read my Prozac book? A huge part of it is about out-of-whack hormones!

I've lived the life and pray you do not let your wife go through what I did. Buy my book. You'll see." I did not feel one iota of guilt for plugging my book. I wrote about my experiences to help other people. I couldn't help my friend and his wife prevent hormonal hell if he didn't at least purchase a copy of my book. Our thoughts on the matter became more of a chat site with people agreeing or disagreeing with what someone before us had posted. These weren't our friends we were corresponding with; these were our mutual friends' friends.

The original question then broke off into subtopics. I was chatting with people that I knew but wasn't friends with. I decided the collecting of friends was a waste of time. I had seventy-odd friends but still only interacted with the original four and a few more.

One day I noticed I got a message in my inbox. I opened it up and sucked in my breath. Jell-O jingle guy was writing to say hello. He too had forgotten how funny I was. It was so great to surmise from other people's chats what I was up to. He asked me about my books, and I responded that 100 percent of the proceeds from my book about my dog went to the Maryland SPCA. He told me my book sounded delightful. That comment instantly transported me back to college. He was such a suck-up then, and he apparently still was. I didn't believe for a minute he used words like *delightful.* I had a book signing in his town, and he promised he would come buy a copy of my books. Mentally I begged him to stay far, far away from me and my books. He was the downside to adding my two cents about the birth control poll. After that little private exchange, I felt the need to take a hot, hot shower to wash away his slimy self. I was not worried in the least about seeing him. I knew he wouldn't come. He didn't.

I was attending a charity event in late spring and needed to wear a bridesmaid's gown. The event was called Bridesmaid Bingo, and the point of the event (besides making oodles of money for at-risk women) was to find a use for those hideous gowns of yesteryear that the brides always swore the bridesmaids would be able to wear out to dinner.

I had long ago gotten rid of those hideous closet space wasters. “I need a bridesmaid’s dress to wear for a charity event,” I posted. Sadly, the response was fairly dismal. People had either gotten rid of theirs too or worried about the fit. I did not care about the fit. In fact, I thought the worse it fit the better it would have been.

After posting my request for about five weeks, I only got one dress. One of my original four had worn it to the same event a few years past. It was perfect. It transported me back to the mid-1980s with its ruffle on the chest and bow in the back. I tried it on, and it looked beautiful. There was no way I could wear a bridesmaid gown that I looked good in! I realized the event was for charity, but the organizers had their tongues firmly inside their cheeks when they came up with the dress code. What bride would ever allow her attendant to look as good as or better than her? Wasn’t that the point? The attendants were supposed to wear unflattering dresses. That was why the bride always said something about the dress being able to be worn again after the wedding. She was so focused on herself and her big day that she never stopped to consider that we bridesmaids would never have been caught dead wearing this unflattering dress twice.

I ran into a parent at my son's school who owned a boutique. I asked her if she had anything "bridesmaidy" and inexpensive I could buy for my charity event. I stressed that I did not want to look good. She understood immediately and told me her store was having a big sale and there was at least one dress that was probably going to work for what I needed. The buyer for the boutique wasn't sure if she was supposed to be offended that I was coming to that store for an ugly dress. I wasn't able to talk my way out of why she should not have been offended. I was only able to offer that the dresses in the boutique were beautiful (and they were), but if I wore one that was the wrong color or an unflattering fit, I would be upholding the unspoken bridesmaid rule of "Thou shalt not look as good as or better than the bride." She was with me on that point and began to show me dresses. One was the dress

I had heard about at my son's school. It had a bow in the back and an asymmetrical hem. Another was one I dubbed "Barbie's bridesmaid." It had an off-white bodice with a bright pink skirt that looked as though it had a mile of crinoline under it. If I were to have sat down, the front of the skirt would have come up to my chin. The buyer and an employee raved at how bad it looked. It sounded so funny! I was shopping in one of Baltimore's best shops for something that made me look bad.

Then I saw it. I had passed over the dress originally because it was really pretty on the hanger. It was pink and orange with a tight bodice and short skirt. There was even a bow in the back. I didn't know why I was going to try it on. The colors were really good for me. I kept thinking about the Barbie dress and the fact that no bride would have her attendant wear off-white. I tried it on, and I looked horrible! I could not believe that something that was so pretty on the hanger would have been so awful on me. The skirt part of the dress had pockets, which I loved. Sadly, the way the pockets were pleated made my rear end look like the broad side of a barn. The back had fabric that looked like it was supposed to have hidden a bra strap, but it was up too high. Above the fabric was a bow that did nothing. I had found my dress!

I posted on Facebook that I had found the most hideous, unflattering bridesmaid dress ever. I also wrote to my friend that her gown was just too pretty for any self-absorbed bride to allow her attendant to wear. I sent it over to a friend of mine who was going with me. I knew the ruffle was going to hit her in just the wrong spot and that gown would be awful for her.

My friend who had lent me the gown wrote that she had looked beautiful in that gown. I believed her. I also knew that she couldn't have been a Bridezilla or an attendant to one and therefore would not have had any idea what it was like to have insulted the bride for looking good.

Angsting over my Facebook Friends

What Facebook friends wrote as their status determined how many people commented back. We all had opinions and were great at giving feedback. I had always gone about my life thinking that if any of my life experiences thus far could be beneficial to anyone else, I would have shared my knowledge. I felt this way about my friends that were not on Facebook as well.

One friend wrote about a mouse. She wanted it out of her kitchen for good. I had to write a comment. "There is no such thing as one mouse. Get an exterminator." She laughed and wrote that there was no need to call in the professionals when she could handle the situation on her own. What to do? "That's what I thought too. In fact, I had Ken go to the hardware store to get one of those containment devices that captured the mouse so we could set it free." She responded that those things didn't work. *I know,* I thought to myself. She didn't need my help, so I went on to connect with other friends.

I couldn't stop thinking about that mouse. I went to bed thinking about it, had dreams about it, and woke up and immediately checked her status in the morning to see how many mice she had at that point. We had had a mouse in our house. It turned into two mice. They bred and had nine babies. Two weeks later those original mice had another litter of nine. At that point, the original nine babies were able to have babies of their own. They did. We had mice all over the place. They were in our bedrooms, the basement, our walls, in the cupboards, and the living room.

I was a total nutcase. My biggest fear was that one would crawl up my pant leg like the old *Tom and Jerry* cartoons. I couldn't eat. I couldn't sleep. All I did was clean up mouse droppings. The exterminators were extremely helpful in keeping the population from growing any further, but we still had many mice running around. One evening I went to the basement to get our stadium seats for a basketball game, and I watched as a bag of Cheetos scurried across the floor. My son saw a mouse and yelled out. That mouse had a heart attack and died.

I went from savior of all living things to maniacally gluing cheese puffs to the traps in order to kill the dirty intruders. I paid my sons five dollars a trap that they found with a dead mouse in it and threw away. They even had their own boxes of latex gloves to use. Ken found a family of mice in a box of old t-shirts I had left down in the basement. They were dead, so he took the box outside and stuck it by our trash cans. A bit later, I went to throw out a bag of trash, and a mouse climbed out of the box and over my shoe. I have never screamed. For some reason, my natural response to horror was to suck in my breath. I hyperventilated.

I begged my husband to let us sell the house. "We'll take one thousand dollars off for every mouse we've had, and the house will sell in a day." I didn't know what was more disgusting, the fact that we had ninety-six mice in our house at one time or that I had bothered to count them.

One day the last mouse was killed. For years after that, whenever I saw a whisper of dog hair blow across the floor, I would freak out, thinking it was a mouse.

My friend did get rid of her one mouse and never had trouble after that. Another friend of mine wrote that he was waiting for some test results from a hospital. I felt the part of me that needs to help others go into high alert. I related to his concerns both as a medical professional and as a parent. Obviously it was a personal matter, but I thought I could help expedite getting the results of the tests. I asked if I could help in any way and wrote that I had a terrible medical scare a few years back and how I went about getting the results.

Privacy laws were good until they weren't. I had heard of parents not ever finding out how their son had died because "it wasn't compliant." Were they kidding? However, privacy laws were a great reason to not have to discuss patients for any reason. That particularly came in handy if an employer was checking up on an employee that was a patient of ours. No matter how they tried to ask a question about that patient, I could only recite, "I'm sorry. The HIPPA laws prevent me from discussing this patient. I could be fined twenty-five thousand dollars for stating anything at all about our patients, and well, if I had that kind of money, I'm sure I could find better ways to spend it." I would get hung up on, but a law is a law. As parents, we wanted to have the privacy laws not be in place for us. It was our child. We could help if we knew what was going on. For most minor children, a form was signed stating that the child and parent agreed to let the parent know about medical concerns. As the children grew older and became teenagers, they did not have to agree to let their parents know what the medical issues and concerns were.

I had many roles as a health care professional. Because our office was small and intimate and human, not automated, I added patient advocate as one of my job titles. I knew some of the ins and outs of filling out and filing paperwork. I privately wrote to my friend and suggested to him ways to get the test results. There was no reason to wait eight days to find out the results of something the technicians had a preliminary result for in a couple of hours. There was still a lot of compassion in the medical field, so it always blew me away that a nurse or doctor or aide of some type didn't remember that they were dealing with a child and that as parents they would have wanted to know the results immediately too. The business end of the medical world was making professionals too edgy to remember the human component.

I couldn't sleep. I wrote to my friend every day asking if the results were in. I couldn't have been helping his stress, but I could be very persistent, in a nice and charming way, and knew I could help him in some capacity. My friend did get the results and everything seemed fine, so I focused my angst elsewhere.

Another friend wrote that he was driving cross-country in a tiny car by himself. I worried for him. I had driven across the country, but I had someone with me out and back. Here was a man with a family, a job, a mortgage, and a dream, and I was writing to him asking if he had his car tuned up and ready to go for the big trip. He wrote that the car was in great shape. "Did you check vital fluids and tire pressure?" Yes, he had. I think he was thinking I was insulting his intelligence, but I was just concerned. I knew that there were certain stretches of desert where if you broke down you were out of luck for about one hundred miles. That had terrified me as a driver; I was terrified as a Facebook passenger.

He didn't update his status for a couple of days. I worried. He wrote that night saying he was in some state in a hot tub. I was relieved. Then I worried again. What if he got electrocuted using his computer in water? He wasn't dumb, I had to remind myself. He updated his status when he got back home. I was so relieved for him and his family. I couldn't wait to read about the trip.

Another friend asked for suggestions about music to download for a long trip she was taking by herself. She didn't say why she was taking the trip initially. We suggested all sorts of music from the '80s primarily, and I had mentioned a new album I liked quite a bit and quoted some of the lyrics for her to read. I called this particular genre "hilarious emo." That's when she wrote that she was going to a funeral. Where was the delete button? I wanted to erase my whole last suggestion. I felt like an idiot, but I was just trying to help. I wrote to her when I thought she had arrived at her destination. She was fine, sad, and tired, but otherwise okay.

Why I Angsted

I was fiddling around on the computer one Friday night when a Facebook friend wrote and asked if all famous authors stayed home on a Friday night. I wrote something snarky back about not having enough of an entourage to bother going anywhere. He was writing from a train on his way to New York. How fun! I wanted to know who was with him and what he was doing in New York. He wrote back that he was alone and meeting a colleague for a social event. That sounded great. I wanted to know where in New York the event was. He replied that he didn't know.

Was he serious? He was taking a train to New York, being picked up and taken someplace that he did not know, and he was fine with it. What if it was a setup? What if there was no social event at all, they were just going to attack him or something?

Why was I doing this to myself? I wondered. My friend was an adult. He was married, had children, and was the CEO of a corporation. He was no dummy. He wrote that he liked taking risks. I hadn't remembered that about him in college, but how would I have known? It wasn't as though he had jumped off the water tower wearing a Superman cape.

He wrote that sometimes taking risks made him happy. The psych major in me wrote something about wondering if people took risks because they were confident and happy or because they were self-doubters and insecure. That was not one of my better subjects, particularly for a Friday night, and he mentioned as much. It was impossible to be cerebral on the same level with a poli-sci major anyway. I wrote down a list of all the reasons I was afraid of risks and the unknown. He was no longer online and did not receive my last message, but when I saw what I had written, I had figured it out.

I angsted about my Facebook friends so I wouldn't think about my own personal fears and regrets. I thought I could help my friends, but I felt fairly certain that, without the aid of anti-anxiety medication and my psychiatrist on speed dial, I couldn't help myself.

What if I were to take a train by myself and not have known what I was doing or where I was going in a specific sense? What if something happened to me? Who would have been me instead of me? What if I went away and never came back? Would my family be okay? Would the dogs get fed and walked? Would my children turn out okay? Would they be clean?

So I thought about it. What would my family have been like without me? I was thinking in a strictly hypothetical way. I was not about to do something stupid and have my family pick up the pieces without me. In a nutshell, my family would have been fine. I had taught them well up to this point. My husband was a great man and father. The dogs would have been fine; even our older dog with pancreatitis would have received his medication when he was supposed to. That was a *eureka!* moment for me. I put a lot of pressure on myself. I always had and didn't foresee a change in that department. I realized that if I sat back and relaxed, I would have been fine too.

That particular Facebook friend was rarely online, and our correspondence was infrequent. I suspected that after my psychologically off-putting subject about risk takers and happiness was posted, I probably would not hear from him again for a while. I was glad we had that chat.

Mom Arms

On the day I turned twenty-five, I stood in front of the full-length mirror and watched as my skin started to sag. I had read enough issues of *Vogue* magazine to know that at the horrifyingly magical age of twenty-five, the quarter-century mark, women began to lose the elasticity of their skin. Coco Chanel had warned that women over the age of twenty-one should no longer wear sleeveless dresses but should opt instead for capped sleeves. This, I supposed, was so women would look their age. I told myself that since I was way too poor to own anything Chanel, real or fun fake, and didn't live in France, I could be sleeveless until I turned twenty-five.

I have a September birthday, and the weather was usually hot. After my depressing self-examination in the mirror, I decided to wear three-quarter-length sleeves. It didn't matter that it was too sultry to wear anything but the lightest of sundresses. I was going to uphold my fashion responsibility and no longer expose my saggy skin arms. I had broad shoulders. In the eighties, I never wore the fashionable shoulder pads seen in shows like *Dynasty;* I didn't need to, though people thought I was anyway. I knew a linebacker-cut person like me was never going to be able to pull off capped sleeves, so three-quarter-length sleeves seemed to me the most sensibly stylish way for a quarter-centurion to go.

It never occurred to me to wear sleeveless shirts or dresses again unless I was at the pool or gym, and then it was because I was so busy covering my bedonkadonk tush that I thought my arms were the much lesser of two evils. It was only when I had my babies and had really muscular baby-arms that I dared expose the upper part of my arms.

My weight had yo-yoed from anorexic thin in 1997 to meaty and curvy in 2001. My grandfather had died the year before, and I turned to food as comfort. I looked comforted all right. We were coming home from family vacation during the summer of 2001, and it was my turn to drive. It was a beautiful day in upstate New York, and we opted to put down the windows instead of blasting the air-conditioning. I had rested my arm on the sill of the window as I was driving. I looked in my rearview window to see if any car was behind me, and that's when I saw it: flab. My tricep area looked loose and large as it hung from my propped-up elbow.

"Why didn't you tell me my arms are fat?" I shrieked to my husband, who was desperately trying to sleep off the hangover we each had from our last night of partying. My husband mumbled something about how beautiful my arms were, and I made a comment that obviously he was still wearing his beer goggles. All the way home during that six-hour drive, I stared at my arm in either the driver's side or the passenger's side rearview mirror.

I cannot believe my arms are so flabby even wearing short-sleeves!

When we got home and unloaded the car, I threw in the first of several loads of laundry and ran up the stairs to look at myself in the mirror while only wearing my underwear. The nap my husband took in the car gave him enough energy to crawl up the steps to take another nap in our bed. "Ken! Look at this!" I screeched. "I have totally let myself go! I drink too much when we go out, I eat the wrong foods, and I obviously don't exercise enough. Just look at me! I'm disgusting!" I wiggled the wibble-wobble under my arms and then put my hands at the place where my legs and buttocks met and lifted the skin up and down. I looked like a flabby old woman, and I was only in my early thirties.

Fast forward a few years to my other issues, and my arms didn't look that bad. I'd had liposuction on my hips, thighs, and flanks, so I was no longer worried about that part of my anatomy. It became my double chin or my "rolly tummy" as the boys called it at the pool one day or that irritating back fat that oozed out above and below the bra strap. I took up tennis, began running, and managed to be so stressed about life in general that I lost about twenty pounds. For the first time, I was actually wearing sleeveless tennis outfits, and I liked the way my arms looked. It didn't matter that I was so underweight that I would get lightheaded and stumble when I looked up to serve. I looked adorable in my tennis togs.

I took a break from tennis, had a bit of an ongoing anxiety attack that became my new workout, and adopted a dog. For the first six months or longer that I had Waldo, he was a very impolite walker. He lunged and pulled and ran and darted at rabbits and squirrels. I needed both arms to pull him back to me to get some so-called control. When a neighbor commented on what a big, strong dog Waldo was, I agreed and mentioned that I might go sleeveless for the first time in fifteen years.

One of my Facebook friends had been a friend since we were teenagers. We both rode horses and swam and lived as close together as two people who lived on farms could. She had always been in phenomenal shape. She had strong, athletic arms and legs that were probably the same circumference as my own, but because mine were not as muscular, hers looked smaller than mine. We had lost touch for about twenty years and then reunited at the grocery store. It turned out we were neighbors within walking distance again. We complimented each other on how great the other looked, but only I was telling the truth. She had the most beautiful arms. She never lost the elasticity. She was only two years younger than me, but I swore she had her fourteen-year-old arms.

We were in and out of touch, mostly bumping into each other while running errands. I found her on Facebook, and we found that to be a more consistent way to communicate. One day she wrote that she rode her bike to the library and back and didn't stop at Dunkin Donuts either way. She then added she was going to work on her "mom arms" so they could feel as worked on as her legs. One of her friends responded with a question mark. Another asked what mom arms were and translated the question mark from the reply above it. My friend wrote back that mom arms were the arms you ended up with when no amount of diet or exercise could get rid of the jiggly part of the upper arm. This was coming from a person who the last time I saw her looked like she could have been on the cover of a number of fitness magazines. I responded that she was probably one of the last people to worry about mom arms since she had such an athletic physique.

She wrote back that although she tried to stay active and busy, a surgery that she'd had the year before had really been hard to recover from, and she was just getting back to a level of fitness she found to be acceptable. Her arms and legs had lost their tone.

It had been about sixteen months that I had had Waldo, and although he was much more mannerly on our walks, I still had a lot of lean muscle mass. I was fixated on some of my other imperfections, such as unwanted facial hair and how my shorts felt too tight across the tush, and had left my arms alone, until that post. I flashed back to the wibble-wobble of the car ride in the summer of 2001. I was still about twenty pounds less than what medical books advised for my height and thought nothing of wearing sleeveless dresses to my sweltering office. We had some patients who felt they could offer what I could only have hoped was meant to be constructive criticism about my weight, height, hair, or outfit, and I brought along a sweater for the day a patient would tell me that my skin was too old and saggy to show that much of my arms.

My friend later posted she was off to Europe for the summer. She was looking forward to going away to new countries, particularly since most of Europe seemed to have praise for soft, fleshy bodies. I went to the beach for a few days of downtime and rode my standup paddle board all around the canal in the back of our house. I would be gone for an hour at a time simply transfixed by all the sea life I could see on those clear days. Most of the days I used my board were calm, but as I got better and more confident in my balance, I went out when it was breezy. Going along with the wind was easy; turning around and heading back was more strenuous. I felt the muscles in my arms and back tightening against the force of the wind.

I saw two women walking down a boardwalk using water bottles as arm weights. I remembered those days well, except I had used an unopened can of soup to do curls whenever I was on the telephone. One woman turned to the other and said that paddling looked like a much more fun way to work arms. They were right! It was exhilarating. It didn't feel like work until later when I peeled off my grimy bathing suit and lifted my arms to wash my hair in the shower.

My younger, soon to be teenage son had invited me to go go-cart racing with him and my husband. I was honored to be included, as I knew his days of being near me were coming to a close. The go-carts were the most uncomfortable things I had been in for a long time. I was always a defensive driver, so I tried to stay out of the way as cars rushed past me and accidentally clipped me in their need to win. We rode cars for an hour, and bruises were beginning to appear on my legs. The sensation I could not ignore, which was even stronger than ache of the welts that were forming on my knees and ankles, was the residual itch of my triceps from where they had jiggled for sixty minutes.

Thanks, Facebook friend … not.

My Facebook Social Experiment

I was amazed at the sheer number of friends some of my friends had. We were talking in the hundreds to near one thousand. I wondered what the quality of friendship was. Would they go to the friend's funeral? Would they drive them to the airport? I didn't think so. There were plenty of jokes that alluded to this fact as well. The bottom line or punch line was that these people were only your friends until you needed money or help moving.

I agreed. Some people who had friended me early on had unfriended me at some point because they wanted to keep their friendship list cohesive.

In fact, the girl who is the title character of this book unfriended me, and I had no idea that she had. Clearly we were not close, but I was still upset that she unfriended me. She was the title of this book! How dare she unfriend me! I should be the one to unfriend her. My college boyfriend dumped me for her, and then *she,* twenty some years later, dumped me. That was just plain wrong. Clearly her age had not helped her gain good taste in friends. I did have a Facebook friend that I helped move. I got to know her a lot more during those few hours of packing and hauling than I had in the two years we stood side by side watching our sons play football together.

A Facebook friend from Florida that I had gone to college with was coming to Maryland for a milestone birthday party. I wanted to see him and knew our mutual friends would too. This guy had about four hundred and fifty friends. I was mutual friends with thirty-five of them. I sent a notice to those people asking what they thought about getting together either in Baltimore or the eastern shore. Word got out, and other friends told their mutual friends. A few times people were inadvertently left out of notifications, but we were able to fix that for the most part.

Facebook had been the perfect icebreaker for us. We knew all the small talk; we could get right into the nitty-gritty of life. We knew what we all were doing in the present tense, thereby eliminating the embarrassment only being able to remember a friend by their college antics. The person that set the fire outside his dorm using the furniture from his room and the common area had actually gone on to marry, have children, and be respected in the community. We wouldn't have to break the ice by asking if he'd started any good fires lately.

One friend said that she wouldn't be able to come to the party because she was moving. She was moving on a Friday at seven at night? That wasn't an acceptable excuse. Come to think of it, the person who said they would not be able to come due to medical concerns didn't have much of an excuse either. After several private chats with this woman and days of peeling away layers, I found out what the problem was. She was fiercely independent and at times bullheaded. She rarely, if ever, asked for help. She had kept us posted as to why she was moving, why her circumstances had changed, and how she was trying to cope with it all. Her friends responded with words of good cheer, offers of help, and places she might like to live within good school districts. I asked her closer to the date of the party what I needed to do to make sure she came to my house. She responded that she didn't know.

I didn't hear from her for a while and continued making plans for our little college get-together. One night I happened to notice she was on Facebook and asked how she was doing. Interestingly enough, most of her three hundred or so friends were unwilling to help her in any way. This independent, I-can-do-it person asked for help for a change, which was really hard for her to do, and some of her so-called friends told her she was a whiner and they thought she had a negative attitude and would be in touch if she had something positive to say. She was completely overwhelmed by life and its curveballs, and when she reached out for help, she got a negative reaction from those very people that she loved and trusted. I was furious. I was also a little Zen and told her that she would know who her true friends were at the end of the move.

I initiated a private conversation between two of her really good friends and a friend of mine and hers that was helping me get the word out about the party. "What would you guys think if I provided the food instead of having people bring a dish to share, and the people who wanted to bring something could contribute instead to helping our friend move with gift cards or the monetary amount they would have spent on a dessert?" A plan was hatched, and soon people who didn't really remember her from college but were Facebook friends of hers offered to bring gift cards to local grocery stores and restaurants to the party for her.

While I did believe that most Facebook friends were just there, in a way, I wanted to prove that Facebook friends could be friends that would help you move, give you money, or drive you to the airport: “real friend” jobs. I wrote notes to the friends that were coming to the party and said I was conducting a Facebook social experiment, and they did not have to participate in any other way than to show up at my house at the allotted date and time. The point was to have a little college reunion; we just happened to have had an opportunity to help someone who needed it.

Our Florida friend was really feeling the distance that separated the two of them. He sent me a private message asking how he could help from almost two thousand miles away. I told him I would find out and let him know. Sure enough, the moving company was more expensive than she thought, and he instantly replied that he was willing to put the move on his credit card. I had given her dates of when I was available to help with whatever she needed to have done. I felt compelled to let her know that my extreme need for order and tidiness might seem a bit off-putting. I told her that my mantra to just about everything was “when in doubt, throw it out." If she wanted to hold on to dear Aunt Lulu's hand crocheted doilies, I would pack them. If she wasn't sure about something, I was almost guaranteed to tell her to get rid of it if she asked what I thought.

I was surprised and delighted when she wrote to me asking to remind her of the days and times I was available to help her. She didn't know what she needed help with because she had her hands in so many moving issues. I told her that I was without my big SUV on the first day, but we could use that time to make piles of what to keep, toss, donate, or sell. I would bring my truck the next day to go to the dump, Goodwill, or consignment stores.

I called her up and told her I was ready to come out to help. I was getting a cab and would be there as soon as I could. She had already done a great job of purging and had six heavy-duty trash bags filled with things that needed to go to the dump. I told her I would ask for a van to pick me up so we would have room to put the trash. I had two transportation companies that I used on a regular basis. The first one was booked, but the second one said they had a van available. I let the dispatcher know that I wanted the van to put bags of trash in to take to the dump. She told me she would send for the van but I would need to talk to the driver myself about taking the bags to the dump.

It was a risk. I would be riding in a van by myself for approximately six miles and be paying a van charge, and it might have been a waste of money. I got into the van and asked the driver if the dispatcher had said anything to him about moving trash. He said he knew nothing about it. I asked him if he knew about Facebook, and of course he did, but he was not on it himself. I explained I was trying to conduct an experiment of sorts. I told him that I would do the lifting and the tossing; I just needed him to drive me to the dump. We got to talking about how you don't really know someone like you thought until you need help. We shared horror stories about how sometimes being nice to family or close friends made us feel used and unappreciated.

I called my friend and said I was on my way and asked her to put the big bags outside so I could load them and take them to the dump before it closed. I was appalled. I didn't get the driver's answer to whether or not he would be willing to go to the dump. Apparently he had said that he would help as soon as I asked, but we got so busy talking and solving the world's problems that I either hadn't heard him or forgot what he said.

We knew which apartment building was hers by the bags of trash that were in the front. We quickly loaded the bags and got to the dump about fifteen minutes before it closed. The man in charge told us which dumpster to use, and off we drove. The dumpster was huge. It was about ten feet high and twenty feet long. "Where's the sliding door?" I asked my driving buddy. He thought it was in the back of the dumpster, but it wasn't. We had to throw the bags, which were pretty heavy, from the ground into the dumpster.

I had my game face on and tossed the bag. I missed. Down it came, landing by my feet. I started laughing. "How do you do this?" I asked. My new friend told me to throw it in higher. I did. It fell. I laughed. He began to laugh, and despite the fact that I had told him he wouldn't need to help me, he needed to help me. I threw the bag again, and it landed on the edge of the dumpster and teetered. I blew the air in the bag's direction hoping that it would go in instead of fall back out. It didn't. It landed by my feet.

My helper had thrown in the other five bags and was waiting for me to get mine in. His tosses were beautiful. He made it look so easy. I was no good. I was doubled over laughing and was not going to be able to throw the bag away. A pickup truck backed in beside us loaded with furniture. "Let's watch how these guys are going to throw furniture into the dumpster," I said to my friend. Two men stood on the bed of their truck and placed the pieces of furniture into the dumpster with no problem. I was going to ask if I could step onto their truck to throw my last bag, but something told me that I shouldn't press my luck getting help from strangers.

My friend threw in the last bag and drove me back to my friend's place. I asked my driver if he had a card. He wrote down his name and told me to ask for him whenever I needed "dumb stuff" done.

The party was a great success. About thirteen of my Facebook college friends came to the house. A couple of them were a little late in coming because they were helping our friend pack some last-minute boxes. By around midnight, the six or so that remained went down memory lane with college stories. They were hilarious, and our laughter filled the air along with the citronella candle haze. The friend who was moving stayed for a longer time than she had hoped but seemed nice and relaxed, having been with some people who loved her for who she was. She stayed up all the rest of the night getting ready for her move, but she took some Facebook breaks before the computer got unplugged.

She was nervous because of the move and the unknown that comes with a new place, but she was no longer worried about the financial burden that moving entailed. Her Facebook friends, her true friends, had helped her with that and left the door wide open for her to come and ask for assistance again.

She sent me a private message at about seven the next morning and asked how she could ever repay me or our Florida friend or anyone else that had shown her such unconditional kindness. "I don't ever think I'll be in a healthy enough financial situation to repay you..." I reminded her of what I had been reminded of from our Florida friend, that we didn't need to be paid *back;* she would one day find someone in a situation who would need her help, and then she would pay it *forward.*

Navigating through Facebook Etiquette

For me, Facebook was an outlet, an opportunity to express my rampant thoughts to my friends. If a comment of mine rubbed someone the wrong way, they would either not respond at all or send me a note in my inbox saying that they took issue with a particular rant. Many of my friends were animal supporters. There were different names for the various organizations, but the fact remained that we all wanted to keep domestic animals safe from abuse or neglect. We all stood on our soapboxes from time to time, adding videos or pictures or articles to our opinions, but we tried to do it without pointing fingers or making other people or groups feel bad.

The People for the Ethical Treatment of Animals had a whole different sort of approach to bringing up the awareness of animal cruelty. Some of the articles and statements they made did point fingers and put blame on people for the conditions of animals. I had the misfortune of meeting a PETA person at one of my book signings. I mentioned that 100 percent of the proceeds from the sale of my book *Finally Winsome* went to the Maryland SPCA. She announced that she was a member of PETA, so I said that she obviously understood how important it was to help animals. She looked briefly at my books and then stared down at my shoes. She told me I was a hypocrite because I was wearing leather shoes and obviously didn't mind killing animals for fashion. Wow. That was personal.

One evening a Facebook friend who started an organization that had children take an oath of kindness toward animals shared an article on her wall about PETA. PETA had started an online group called "The PETA Files," which shared snippets of their latest rants to anyone who cared to read them. I cracked up laughing when I read the name "The PETA Files" out loud. It sounded like that they would have done anything to help animals, including harming children. I responded to my friend that it served those "psycho advocates" right to have such a misleading name. Someone wrote a comment after mine saying that she agreed the name of the group was dumb but she was one of those "psycho advocates." I wrote back to her in her inbox and said that she didn't sound like a psycho. The experiences I had in the past with PETA pests was when they had gone to opera houses and thrown red paint on women in fur coats or the experience with the woman at the book signing. Those people had no idea they were psycho advocates, so they would have never admitted to it. So we chatted back and forth for a while and realized we had other things in common, and we friended each other.

While I was at work one day, a friend of a patient asked if I was on Facebook. I said that I was indeed and loved every minute of it. He said that he just joined and that he was going to go home and request me as a friend. He almost pleaded that I become his friend since he didn't have many yet. Sure enough, about an hour later, there was a friend request from this guy. The last thing I wanted to do was to become friends with him, not because I didn't like him, but because he was a friend of one of our patients, and quite frankly, patient stories made for some of my snarkiest comments on Facebook. I left the request hanging in the air for a couple of days as I tried to figure out how to ignore it. Finally, I bit the bullet and hit the "Ignore" button.

A few days later there was another request to be his friend. I understood that logic. He probably thought he had done it wrong and tried the request again. I'd been there. I got that if someone had not become my friend it was because they didn't get the request. Why would anyone say no to me? I was very choosy in who I wanted to ask to be my friend, so it was a done deal and just a matter of time for them to be my friend. So I ignored his request again and went on with my day on Facebook.

A couple of weeks after my last press of the "Ignore" button for being this guy's friend, he came into the office with the patient. He asked me if I got his friend request. I said I had. He mentioned that he may have sent the request more than once because he was still trying to figure out how to navigate his way around Facebook. I told him that I couldn't be his friend. He looked so hurt when I said it, so I went into my best "it's not you, it's me" explanation of how I was really inappropriately rude and gross at times to let off steam. I told him the truth—I was not the friendly person he knew me as in my professional environment. He looked relieved to know it wasn't him and said that he was really surprised because I seemed so nice.

For whatever reason, I was becoming friends with some movers and shakers in the community. One person I requested as a friend was a dare on my part. I did not think he would accept me because he was a member of the media and had interviewed me once. It had not gone well. He readily accepted. Maybe he had lost a dare of his own. One of the many articles that was written about Facebook was by a news columnist who said that he would become friends with anyone who asked him. *That was creative,* I had thought at the time. *I'm not going to be friends with someone who will accept anyone as a friend.* That was dumb. I prided myself on my discrimination.

This columnist wrote some great stuff that I had commented on from time to time via e-mail. When his dog died, I sent him a copy of my book about Winn. It was way too soon after his loss to read it, but I told him to hold on to it for one day when he was ready. He wrote me a letter thanking me for my kindness. The book made its way around the newsroom, and I got a call from another columnist who wrote articles pertaining to life with dogs. He wanted to interview me, but he was leaving the paper and starting his own business. He took down my schedule of book signings for that fall and said he would come out to one of them and interview me during a signing if I wasn't too busy.

This person was probably one of the sweetest men I had ever met. We chatted for a while at a bookstore, and he took some pictures. That was actually pretty cool because it generated a lot of buzz around my table. He was very involved in the Baltimore area animal shelters and often posted on his blog about upcoming events for these groups. When he created a fan site for his blog on Facebook, I signed on immediately. He became my friend too. I suggested friends of mine from animal shelters in the region and on the eastern shore. They all became friends with each other.

Because of the newspaper and other local media connections I had, I decided to request the columnist who would befriend everyone as my friend. I didn't do it to put another feather in his cap. I honestly thought we would have some things in common through our friends. I sent out the request and forgot about it.

A few weeks later, I checked to see if there were other people I could add as friends. A lot of people were mentioned as potential friends, but I didn't see the connection because we had no friends in common. As I continued to look, I was surprised to see that the newspaper person I requested as a friend was suggested as someone I should request as a friend. I was curious about that because I had assumed if someone ignored someone else as a friend, the suggestion would never be made again; so I requested him as a friend and waited.

Every couple of days I would search his name to see if we were friends. A little notice came up saying that the friendship was "pending." I went back to my regular Facebook ways until the next time I'd check and see the friendship was still pending. I wondered what in the world he would have to think about. He was friends with everyone, so what was the hold-up? I checked back again a week or so later, and the notice had changed from "friendship pending" to "add as friend." It appeared that this columnist was willing to accept anyone as a friend, *except* for me!

I did the only thing I could think of at that moment. I went onto my wall and wrote, "My friendship request was ignored by someone who said in a newspaper column that he would become friends with anyone who requested him. I don't know whether this is an all-time low or high." Of course, there were plenty of opinions.

Liking Something

There is another etiquette slippery slope on Facebook besides ignoring a friendship request. It's the "like" button. When friends updated their status, sometimes there was no real response needed other than something along the lines of "good for you" or "keep it up," so there was the option to "like" something someone put on their wall. A thumbs-up showed up in the comment section with the name of the person liking it. People had variations of "like this." If someone wrote that they were having a particularly awful day, a friend might write that they "DISlike this." I was known for asking "Where's the 'love it' choice?" or "I L-O-V-E this!" if a post was really great.

Liking something was fairly cut and dry among friends, but if a fan site had posted a statement or blog, liking that could be easily taken out of context. Along with the rest of Baltimore, I was a huge Ravens fan. During the preseason and season, I ate, drank, and breathed football. It was an obvious choice for me to become a fan of the Baltimore Ravens' Facebook page. The site was one of my favorites for information. I read what was posted and could spew out the information to others and really look like I knew what I was talking about.

One day the Ravens' site posted that one of the preseason players, who ended up being cut from the team, had died. Almost instantly, ten people posted that they "like this." Several others felt the same way. I could not believe how incredibly insensitive and inappropriate it was to like that someone died. I didn't even bother with the comments people had written. There was no cause of death at that point, so I went on to other Ravens' postings. The next day the Ravens' site stated that the former Raven had committed suicide. Three people said that they "like this" before the comments were posted. These comments I did read. Most of the responses were variations on the fact that fans' thoughts and prayers were with the family. One mentioned that he knew the player personally and never guessed for a minute that there were any problems beneath his upbeat personality. One comment was particularly profound and seemed to sum up what other readers were thinking. The poster mentioned how important it is to live each day to the fullest because no one knows what is going to happen.

I went up to the "like this" section and clicked on it. To my shock, the person who made such a thought-provoking statement was one of the "likers." I sent her a message in her inbox. I simply asked her how she could like that the Raven committed suicide and write something so different. I didn't know this woman other than she was a fan of the Ravens, so I figured I had nothing to lose by asking her. She could easily delete my question if she thought I was out of line. She didn't, though. She responded and wanted to know who I was judging her. She asked me if she was not entitled to her own opinion. She then went on to say that she liked that the truth had come out that it was a suicide. She then added a new response and thanked me for asking her why she felt the way she did instead of assuming that she was a cold, heartless person.

Because Facebook is what it is, there is no way to know a person's tone of voice, especially someone you don't know in the real world. I quickly wrote back that I was not out to judge anyone. I saw her profile picture, which showed her with a huge, beautiful smile. She seemed really nice, in my opinion. I told her that. I said that I felt safe asking her for some strange reason and that I had suspected she was "liking" that the cause of death was posted and not the cause itself. I said that I thought it would have been much easier for the family to discover that the football player had some underlying medical condition that had gone undetected. I wanted to end our conversation on a more upbeat note, so I asked her if she was going to an upcoming event for Ravens' fans and meeting some of the players. I admitted that I wanted one of the wide receivers on the team to teach me his special dance.

She wrote back that she had a family member who had committed suicide, and the guilt that the family felt was overwhelming at times. She said that her faith was helping in some of the tough times she had and that she actually had a prayer group the night of the Ravens' fan event. She wished me well and said she hoped I learned the dance and closed by saying that she would pray for God to keep me close. I wrote one last thing that I thought she might need to know. I told her that my own father had committed suicide when I was fifteen, and I thought it was my fault because we had gotten into a huge fight just a few weeks before he died. I thanked her for sharing her story.

In some instances, the "like this" button is not an appropriate response. I felt glad that I took the risk and asked someone who had liked something why. It was easy to talk to a stranger who was connected by a love for the Baltimore Ravens football team.

My Turn to Need Help

I don't know how long I'd been a "fixer" instead of a "feeler." At some point in my life I had put my emotions on hold and started acting and not reacting in situations. There had been a turning point in my life when I had figured out that spazzing out over a problem or unforeseen roadblock did not solve anything and that having a fit of hysteria wasted precious time I could have been using to find an alternate solution.

Just about everyone I knew had a pet peeve about waste. Some people used the back side of faxed spam in their printers. Some drank water out of a reusable cup or bottle to reduce waste of plastic. All of us, at one time or another, were warned by our parents about wasting food. My big waste issue was time. I could never get time back that I had lost. I tried to make the most of my waking hours, and when I slept fitfully, I felt guilty for wasting perfectly good sleep time.

Reacting to an unexpected situation wasted time, I thought. Because of that, I was usually asked to handle problems that seemed enormously emotional for anyone else. One day I came home from picking the boys up from school. As soon as I opened the front door, I smelled this disgustingly foul odor. The kids ran upstairs to get away from it. It took me a nanosecond to find the source; Lucky had gone to the bathroom all over the kitchen floor. There were poop splatters on the walls, the oven, and the chairs. I stood in the threshold and stared. I didn't move. What seemed like hours later, I exclaimed out loud, "Oh my God! What do I do? Where do I start? What happened here? What is this? What do I *do?*"

My normal self would have stated the obvious that there was a huge mess to clean up and done it. I couldn't think. I couldn't act. I could, however, Facebook. "I am in a situation that is so bad that for the first time that I can remember I did not act but instead reacted," I posted on my wall. Then I went back to the kitchen to survey the damage again and opted to take Waldo for a walk. I was hoping that the mess Lucky had left would begin to solidify by the time we got back home. It hadn't, so I checked Facebook. I had a ton of comments ranging from "Are you hurt?" and "Do you need me to call 911?" to "That doesn't sound good," and "Sounds like you're having one of my days." I responded that we all were safe and unharmed.

I went to clean up the mess. It was awful. I tried blotting the floor with paper towels that, contrary to popular belief, were *not* the "quicker picker upper." I didn't count how many rolls of paper towels I used. The floor was a sea of brown. Finally I could see the floor again. I mopped the floor with hot water, changed the mop-head and used hot water with floor cleaner, and then changed the mop-head again. The kitchen smelled like lemon.

I put on another pair of rubber gloves and went down to scrub and sanitize the utility sink.

I went back to Facebook and posted the brand of paper towel I used only picked up certain things quickly and not what I was using it for. A friend commented back, "Is it blood?" I wrote back, "The only way I can think to describe it is 'tinkle-poopie.'" The comments I got after that were hilarious and way too gross to print here.

That problem was awful and overwhelming to me. I got through it okay. Venting on Facebook certainly helped, as did my friends' "doggie diapers" comments.

On another occasion, I had a huge problem; it was me. Tim's birthday was on a weekday, and he knew that he would have a real celebration on the weekend. Ken had a board meeting that he could not get out of, and I had back-to-school night for Tim's school. I would have blown it off normally, but since Tim was in his first year of middle school, I felt strongly that I should attend. I told myself that I would make it up to Tim later that evening.

His school had capped the evening at one hour. *I'll be home by eight fifteen and be able to do something with Tim before he goes to bed,* I justified to myself. I was at a red light and posted on my wall, via my cell phone, "I feel like the worst mother in the whole world right now." I went to the meeting, and to my dismay we were not going to be adjourned until nine thirty. I posted on my wall, "I suck worse than the Pittsburgh Steelers."

I was morose. I was also being rude, choosing to play on my cell phone rather than listen to the principal of the middle school. I told a couple of friends that I really did not want to be at the meeting since it was Tim's birthday. A couple people suggested that I sneak out a little early. One person said she was only staying until eight. She didn't want to leave her kids at home on a school night in case she was needed for homework help alongside her husband. As soon as the closing bell rang, it took all of my self-restraint to not mow down the people in front of me in an effort to speed home before Tim went to bed.

I glanced at my phone at a red light. “No one could ever suck like the Steelers,” responded a friend. We hardly ever exchanged messages, so this was a surprise.

“I do. I missed my son’s birthday to go to back-to-school night. Tim said as I was leaving that this was the worst birthday he ever had.”

“Buy him a BB gun. He’ll forgive you instantly.”

“He actually made out pretty well in the gift department. He got tickets to see one of his favorite performers play and tickets to the Ravens and Broncos game. All he wanted was to go out to dinner and have his day acknowledged.”

“Didn’t you wish him a happy birthday this morning?”

The light changed, so I put down my phone and drove until I got the next red light. “Yeah. And I got him his own box of Berger cookies, which he informed me he now hates.”

“Sometimes birthdays have to be disappointing to make the other ones good.”

My friend was no longer online after that, which was just as well because I wanted to get home and tuck Tim into his bed. He hardly ever wanted me to do that for him anymore, so I made sure I was available at bedtime in case I was needed. I went to say good night to Tim, and he rolled over and asked me why his birthday was so bad. I told him that some days things didn't work out the way we wanted. I reminded him that he was a super special guy and life sometimes got in the way of fun things. I promised we would take him out to dinner the following night and mentioned the upcoming events he would see.

I went back downstairs and got on Facebook. I wrote to my friend that his wise thought about birthdays was exactly what I needed to hear, and I thanked him for the Facebook buddy-hug. Tim's birthday could only get better after that.

Facebook as a Forum

I had a knack for saying just about anything I felt on my Facebook wall. My intentions were never to offend, only to state observations. My friend list exploded overnight with a new group of people that were also published authors. Because they were a new audience, I encouraged them to be a fan of my books rather than my personal friend. I put the message out that my comments were never meant to be harmful but they were snarky, and I had an odd perception of the world that people who did not know my tone of voice in real life might have thought was mean.

I became more of an observer of other friends' comments and life happenings and added my own thoughts here and there. Instead of starting my day with my status, I began using the “like” option so people knew I was on Facebook, only without any pithy comments. One Friday I noticed that I liked a friend’s link to a Web site, but I didn’t remember doing so. I went back to the link and saw that she had added two more links to her wall. I was notified that I liked all of the links even though I had not read any but the one. The one link that came up was an ad for Craig’s List, notifying the public of a lost dog that was found.

This dog was not just lost; he was sick, emaciated, filled with infections, and looked as though there might not have been much more life to him. My friend who had posted the picture of the dog was also on Facebook at the same time, and I wrote to her that I needed more information on the dog right away. She responded that she didn’t know what I could do but wrote to a friend of hers requesting that person and I become friends for the sake of the dog. My original friend bowed out of the dialog, and my new friend and I discussed the awful situation and possible ways that I could help.

The person who posted the ad was a coworker of hers. He took it upon himself to help the dog. After calling various shelters and animal hospitals, he found a vet that could see the dog and assess the situation later in the day. My new friend asked if I thought that having the dog see a vet in the late afternoon was a good idea. I had no idea. I didn't want to overhaul whatever ideas were in place; I just wanted to know how I could help. My new friend gave me the name and cell phone number of the man who was saving the dog. She also gave me the name of the veterinary hospital that was going to help. There was no phone number, so I Googled the name and found that they were on Facebook.

I became a fan of their site and found the phone number listed with the information. I called the number that was listed on Facebook and got a busy signal. Over and over I dialed to receive the monotonous beep that the line was in use. Finally, about twenty minutes later, I was able to get through to the hospital. When the woman answered the phone, I asked her if she knew anything about a dog that was left to die in the street that was coming in at four o'clock. She knew exactly whom I was referring to and mentioned that the phone had been ringing off the hook from people who saw the man's plea on Facebook to get donations to help the dog. The hospital had told the man that they would assess and treat the dog with the donations that came in. She said that within twenty minutes hundreds of dollars had been donated via credit card. I said that I wanted to do the same and gave her the amount and my credit card information. When she heard my amount she wanted to know why I wanted to help. I explained to her that my goal in life was to start a foundation that would pay for surgery or care of sick domestic animals. I wanted to help pet hamsters and horses and everything in between. I felt very strongly that no one should have to euthanize a pet solely because they were unable to pay for the care. So I added that I didn't have a foundation yet but I couldn't sit idly by, watching animals die.

We hung up so the many other callers could try to get through with their donations. We had written each other's name down so we could friend each other on Facebook in order to keep tabs on the dog. The man taking responsibility very kindly uploaded photos of the dog once they were in the veterinary hospital. The dog was standing, apparently having found enough energy after eating a hearty meal and drinking water. Both the dog's custodian and the receptionist reported on their walls that the dog was a mess. His face was cut as though he had been in some dog fights. Some of the cuts were extremely infected. At first glance, the vet wasn't sure that the dog was going to be able to keep one of his ears. The dog's blood and stool were sampled, and X-rays were taken. Other than a couple of nasty infections, the dog was in much better shape than he appeared. He was about ten to twelve years old, malnourished, and in need of vaccinations and was scheduled a two-week follow-up appointment.

A neighboring independent pet store donated a bath and food for the dog. The man took the dog to his home where he lived with a couple of housemates and another dog. He wrote that he was armed with food and medicine and was able to take care of the dog for a little while, but he was unable to take the dog in full time. Responses came back from around the United States. The man had done more than enough already, and there were so many other people who wanted to help as well. The man posted videos of him walking the dog with his own pet and mentioned how social the stray was to both humans and other dogs.

I became very attached to the dog. There was something in that first photo of him on the cold, wet streets of Baltimore that spoke to me. It was a great story, to be sure, but the dog had the saddest eyes I had ever seen. The dog had almost given up, and the man got to him in a nick of time. I wrote privately to the man several times over the course of the week to see if he needed food or supplies or if there was anything else he needed to continue providing a safe and secure environment for the dog. He wrote that he would let me know. He posted an ad on Petfinder.com to see if anyone was interested in adopting the dog. I posted the ad on my page and added that the dog still needed follow-up care and was ten to twelve years old. I implored that whoever took the dog in be willing to commit their time to the dog. No one knew how long he had been on the streets, but his so sad eyes told a story of a dog who very badly needed to be really special to the right person.

I hadn't heard about the dog for a couple of days and went onto the man's wall to see if there were any new pictures. I really only wanted to see the dog's eyes. Did they have hope? Would they have hope? I saw a post that he had exchanged with another friend of mine that I knew from the Maryland SPCA. I inferred that the two were making arrangements for the dog to come out and meet my friend. I wrote to them both privately asking if the dog was going to have a forever home on my friend's horse farm. She wrote back and said that she was going to adopt the dog after he had finished with his vet care. Because she knew how ebullient

I could be, she warned me that I could not make this information public. I promised I wouldn't say anything on Facebook.

My friend wrote later saying that the visit went really well. She and the dog needed each other. She was perfect for him. I told her that I had gotten attached to the dog and was glad there was going to be a happy ending for everyone. As I wrote to her, I could feel my eyes misting over. The ending could have been very different for this dog, but because of a simple link that I had said I liked without knowing what it was and the way the story and news snowballed about the dog's dire situation, all through Facebook, there was a happy ending for so many of us.

The dog did not end up living on the farm as planned. He missed the man that had saved him, and the man missed the dog. The last I heard, the man went to the farm to pick up the dog and keep him permanently.

Unfriending

I had become friends with many authors; some used the same publishing company I did, and some did not. Someone started a group for writers. It was filled with tips about how to market a book, where to buy a book, where book signings were going to be held, and the location of upcoming workshops. I enjoyed the group and had used it to post my own questions and concerns, as well as comment on other others'. The publishing company I use is a Christian one. I like that. I didn't know scriptures by heart and probably worshiped a little differently than some of my coauthors, but I had faith and liked the relationship I had with God.

A couple of the authors were ministers and had words of encouragement for any situation. I loved that. Their advice to be patient and listen to God's will was peaceful to read and also a sharp contrast from my own perils of wisdom, which were funny, irreverent, and usually the things that people thought to themselves but would never express publicly. I was a serious author, but I didn't take myself seriously.

I knew some of the authors in the group were hoping to strike it rich with their books. There were movie deals being brokered and interviews being given. My situation was different. Yes, I wanted my books to sell. Yes, I wanted Reese Witherspoon to play me in the movie based on my Prozac book; if the movie didn't make it to the silver screen, I was more than thrilled to have Kelly Ripa play me for the television version. My profits would start an animal foundation to help offset the high costs of domestic animals who needed surgery but whose owners were unable to afford the care.

I missed a lot of the topic discussions, but I did enter into the middle of one when an author posted that she could barely afford to buy a cup of coffee and did not appreciate some authors using the group site to push book sales. She wrote that she didn't mean to be rude but if she wanted to buy the books that were available she would. She had her own financial issues and didn't need to know that if an author didn't sell a book the bank was going to foreclose on their house. There was shameless self-promotion, and there was desperation.

The poster had an excellent point. We were all just trying to sell our books and get the word out about them. There was no need to guilt anybody into buying a book. I responded to her post by saying that ranting was free and she should continue to do so. I mentioned how some of us did book swaps where we sent each other a copy of our book and then put a review on the Amazon or Barnes and Noble Web sites. Except for the shipping, we could read each other's books for free. She loved my idea, and I offered to send her my two books in exchange for her one. I then introduced her to another writer with whom I'd become very friendly. Pretty soon the three of us were posting replies to group questions in a way that was helpful and hilarious. We cracked each other up and soon took our conversations to our friend site.

One day a conversation went wrong. Since we typed our responses in front of a computer, no one could tell for sure what our tone or body language was saying. Innocent comments were taken out of context. A simple apology and an admission that how something was read was not how we intended it to sound was usually enough to put things back on track. One author thought some of our comments were directed to her personally. Like many of us are at one time or another, she was concerned about her dwindling number of book sales. She lamented that she only sold one book at a recent signing. She had generated a lot of interest, and people had been milling around her table and talking to her, but they didn't buy anything. I responded that she should be happy that she sold one of her books and that the people standing around her table were getting information about her and the book. Although sales were weak that day, interest had been generated, and her next signing could sell more books. I really meant my comment to be uplifting; selling one book was better than selling no books.

She took my words to mean that I thought she was ungrateful for her one sale. She interpreted that I implied she was being greedy and unrealistic. She then went on to say that maybe there was no hope for her as an author and her dream had just been a big waste of money that she did not have. Her reply became, in my opinion, a cry for help. She seemed unstable and fragile mentally. I was worried for her and sad that my words were so misconstrued.

I wrote privately to one of my author friends and asked her what I should do to take back my comment. She told me not to worry about it. She said she had been following all the author posts and that she had tried to help the author with words of encouragement too. She told me that the author she was trying to help wrote back some really mean and inappropriate things about not knowing the whole situation and being quick to judge. I asked her what she did in return, and she wrote, "I had to unfriend her." My friend could not take the negativity this author was posting and had to get away from it. I had never unfriended anyone and asked what happened when she did. My friend wrote back that the person she unfriended wrote her an e-mail stating what an awful and fair-weather person she was and how my friend didn't have any problem being her friend when all was right with the world, but the day she had a bad day, *poof*, the friendship was over.

A group of authors had been established so we could bounce ideas off of each other, and it became nasty. I wrote back to my friend that there were so many ministers in the group; had she written to them about how to handle this person before unfriending her? She had indeed, and they agreed that if the relationship did not feel right, it was wise to end it. I thought about that.

I am a "fixer," not a "feeler." If this woman was thinking about doing something drastic because of a comment of mine that she inferred, I couldn't help her. If I tried to help this woman but she ended her writing career and shut herself off from the world anyway, I would have felt terrific grief and guilt. So, after thinking it through and praying over it, I decided for my own well-being that I had to unfriend this author who misconstrued my words. I had to walk away from the toxicity for my well-being. I did feel a little guilty, but I felt remarkably free. Although she and I were no longer friends, I did read her comments on the author site. Eventually she just went away, never to be heard from again. I wondered about her, but someone wrote that she couldn't take the pressure of having to get by one book sale at a time and started looking for consistently paying jobs. She was the only person I had ever unfriended.

Death and Dying on Facebook

"I lost my best friend today," a friend of mine posted on his wall. The family dog needed to be euthanized. It was almost as heartbreaking to read as it was for him to write. The comments poured in to my friend and his family. There must have been over thirty people who expressed their condolences. This was Facebook at its finest. My friend came to the right forum for comfort. Because we were all separated by our computers and not together in real life, we were all able to share our emotions more openly because no one would see as we tried to hold back the tears.

"My dear, sweet horse couldn't fight any longer," another friend posted at a different time. The horse situation was not as surprising as the dog's because my friend had been keeping us posted for months on her oversized pet: something my other friend chose not to do with his dog. This horse was a complete goof. The predicaments he got himself into were more human than equine. She posted pictures as proof in case we thought she was sniffing the rubbing liniment. When the veterinarian needed to be summoned to her farm, my friend let us know on Facebook. There was nothing we could do or say, but we all prayed for peace and comfort and steady hands for the vet. It was awful.

A friend who fostered homeless cats and fed the feral ones that would not be caught posted that one of them had died. She was sure that the cat had been killed somehow because of its position when she found it. My friend was devastated and angry. Here she was, just one person, trying to make lives better for these stray cats, using her own grocery money to buy food for those kitties, who had to become a back alley vigilante to make sure nothing happened to any of the other feral cats. It was gut-wrenching to read because she treated the cats like they were her own pets.

"I watched my best friend from middle school take her last breath today," mourned a friend. She was the first friend of mine who had posted a death of a person. She later wrote that watching someone die was a life-altering thing. She had felt such a tremendous amount of anguish and guilt for not being more active in her friend's life after they went to different high schools. The dying friend was at peace and had apparently come to terms with her finality. My Facebook friend felt awful for gleaning comfort from her friend instead of providing it.

"How's your mom doing these days? Is she home from the hospital?" I had inquired of a friend who had kept a few of us posted about the ups and downs of her mother's health. Some days had much happier posts than others. I didn't know or remember the specifics of the situation, and I didn't want to ask for fear of upsetting my friend. I had heard from a mutual friend that the mother was about to be discharged and sent home. I almost fell out of my chair when I read that the mother had unexpectedly passed away. It took me a few minutes to come back to my senses and offer my condolences. She asked me what I thought about her posting the fact that her mother had passed away on Facebook. I offered that I thought she would get a lot of comfort hearing from old friends. My friend did make a statement on her wall about her mother, and the responses came pouring in. There were pages of comments written on her wall and to her in a private forum. Many of the comments were thanking my friend for letting them know on Facebook. It was easier to read the terrible news than to get a phone call about it. My friend later commented that it was easier to read the comments people left because she could log off of Facebook when the posts got too hard to read.

"My thoughts and prayers are with the family. She was a dear, dear lady." I read that post three times. I never, ever, in a million years thought I would read on Facebook about someone close to me dying. I had just randomly read peoples' posts after I logged onto Facebook. I was definitely not expecting to see that anyone, much less someone I had known almost my entire life, had died. My friend from the SPCA who unsuccessfully tried to adopt the stray dog found in the street had been the one who posted her comment in such a random way.

"What?" I wrote as a response. How could this have happened? Why was I finding out on Facebook? This woman was someone I had cherished since I was seven years old.

My friend didn't respond as immediately as I had hoped, so I called my mother on the phone. "Mom, Is it true? Did our closest neighbor and family friend die? I read about it on Facebook."

My mother was waiting for me to get home so she could call me there instead of telling me the tragic news on my mobile phone. She was afraid I'd crash the car. "It never even occurred to me you would have heard about this unexpected tragedy on Facebook. I think I hate Facebook." *Me too,* I was thinking.

After I hung up from my mother, I went to my friend's Facebook inbox. "Never mind. I talked to my mother and got the details. I am so shocked that I'm not even sad yet." She wrote me back and said that she didn't know any of the details, so I told her what I knew, which was basically that our friend's passing was not expected; it was sudden and was exactly how she wanted to go. She was young, healthy, and on vacation, which were three of her criterion if she got to choose how she got to die.

As I found out details about the memorial celebration, I posted them to my friend. She was going to be out of town for the holidays for the memorial, something our friend would have highly approved of. I went to the memorial service. There were hundreds and hundreds of people there. For hours people shared hilarious and heartwarming anecdotes about this amazing woman. I came back home and posted on Facebook, "I just came back from the funnest memorial party ever. Your friends are sick, just sick!"

I had gotten over the fact that I learned about our close friend's untimely death on Facebook. In the end, it didn't really matter how I found out. I would have reacted with the exact same shock and disbelief if my mother had called me. It was months before I finally put away the SPCA calendar that had my Waldo as the March photograph that I was planning to give her for Christmas.

Please Pray for Us

Not too long ago, both of our dogs got a stomach bug. We figured they both got into the same thing but could not figure out what it was. Waldo was feeling better before Lucky was. Lucky seemed to be very uncomfortable. I posted on Facebook that I didn't know if I should take Lucky to the pet ER or wait until morning for his regular vet to open. Lucky didn't have a fever and was drinking water, so we decided to keep him at home for the night. He could not find a comfortable position and spent a better part of the night looking for a different way to lie down, moaning as he did.

The next morning I dropped the boys off at their schools and took Lucky over to the vet. I spoke with the staff and told them what had been going on with Lucky for the last twenty-eight hours. Lucky had not had anything to drink since waking up, and it was apparent that he was becoming dehydrated. I said to the staff that Lucky needed to be evaluated and given IV fluids. At that point, Lucky was too weak to walk, so I carefully lifted him out of the car and gently passed him to the tech, who carried him into the office.

I got to work and immediately went onto Facebook. "Please pray for Lucky. We don't know what's wrong with him, but he is very sick." In an instant, comments were posted from my friends who wanted to know what was wrong and how they could help.

We had suspected that Lucky had eaten a sock. This was a naughty habit he'd been unable to break since being a puppy. By the grace of God, the socks had always passed, but since he had vomited, we wondered if the sock was lodged somewhere in his stomach. I had, unfortunately, picked the worst day to just drop off Lucky without an appointment.

The vet who was on duty was by himself and had a completely jam-packed day. Lucky was going to have to wait all day before he was seen. I didn't know what to do or think. I didn't want to take Lucky to the pet ER so he could be treated immediately as the vet suggested. I thought it would be way too stressful for him. I said I would pick him up after work and take him to the ER then. "I don't know what to do. I am unable to think, and the vet is overwhelmingly busy. Please pray for us." Again, the comments came pouring back:

"We are praying for you."

"We are keeping Lucky in our thoughts."

"Have faith and patience. Everything will be okay. I can just feel it."

I needed to get out of the office and clear my head. I went to the car, and my phone rang. It was the vet calling. Everything was under control. The other vet (who we considered to be Lucky's vet) was coming in to assess the situation. X-rays had been taken. I ran a couple of errands and came back to the office and posted on Facebook, "Your prayers are working. Lucky's vet is coming in on his day off to see what's wrong. Thank you all for praying. Please don't stop."

The comments came in instantly.

"Will do."

"You got it."

My cousin had just finished reading my book about Waldo and wrote that she would definitely pray for Lucky since she knew exactly what a special part of our family he was. For a while, there were no updates. I got off Facebook and did some work.

Just as we were about to close the office for the day, Lucky's vet called and said that an IV had been started and the X-rays showed there was an obstruction of some sort. They were going to run a couple more tests on him to see if the object would pass on its own before deciding to operate. I hung up and went back onto Facebook. "Lucky will more than likely have surgery. Given the fact that he is weak and underweight, there is a significant risk. If Lucky does not have surgery, he will die. Please keep my husband in your thoughts. I don't know what he'd do if anything happened to the Luckmeister."

I didn't get back on Facebook until late that same evening and was shocked to see that there were over seventy messages and posts from people who were keeping Lucky and my husband in their thoughts and prayers. One friend wrote that he would keep the vet in his prayers. For some reason, that post made me burst into tears. I'd been trying to keep my emotions in check and not cry about Lucky, but my friend's post was so simple yet so important. I'd forgotten to ask people to pray for the vet. Jeez Louise!

Lucky ended up needing surgery. The X-ray was not clear, but Ken and I were almost positive that a sock was causing the obstruction. Indeed, when the vet called to let us know Lucky was awake and alert, we were informed that it was a sock, a man's tube sock, that had done the damage. Of course we took a picture of it and posted it on Facebook with the caption, "Eeeeewwww, Lucky!" He recovered nicely and was monitored at the vet's office for several days. We were able to visit him, and I kept posting his progress on Facebook. Friends I had only heard from once or twice since joining Facebook were sending their thoughts and good wishes our way. I knew I could have handled Lucky's tummy trauma on my own, but I felt so fortunate that I had a support system.

My Facebook Experience

I had been on Facebook for a year. Facebook had changed its format several times since I joined, and I liked the original format the best. It seemed to me that with each change I got information that I didn't care about and missed posts that I did care about. The Maryland SPCA donated copies of my book to people who adopted animals on a certain day, but I missed that post because someone else's post about needing a pitchfork in Farmville came up instead.

There were still a lot of things I didn't understand about Facebook, but when I asked how to get rid of people's posts about farms, fish, hugs, hearts, and all the other applications I could not have cared less about, I found out that I could delete all of that nonsense and still keep the person as a friend. That was important to me. I could engage in conversations with people I genuinely liked and cared about and tidy up the things that got posted on my wall. A friend deleted a lot of friends that she deemed "too much work" and sent a post saying that she was cleaning house and not to take it personally. I got to stay as a friend although I had never met her in real life. I knew her because I said something to a friend about PETA that her sister had found offensive and the sister and I became friends. Facebook was weird like that.

It did give me the courage to take stock of my friends. Did I need to have so many? Was it a popularity contest? I had friends in the triple digits, but as I categorized them, I had to look on their profile to remind myself how I knew them. If I unfriended people I never heard from, would they be unfriended from my author site as well? Could I get those people to unfriend me but become a fan of my books? I knew that whether I had five hundred friends or my original core four plus a few more, I knew who my honest-to-goodness friends were.

A year later, I couldn't even believe I cared that the boyfriend stealer of this book's cover unfriended me. I couldn't believe how paranoid I was when the boyfriend decided to get off Facebook and leave no trace of other social arenas. What was wrong with me? Why was I so insecure? I don't remember being especially nice to either one of them in college. Did I want to be the unfriender and not the unfriended?

The fact remains, I love Facebook. It is probably the best social outlet for me. I can catch up on what's going on without being on the telephone all night. Through Facebook, I'm continuing my quest to clean up my part of the world and do good things for animals.

There are some things I would do differently if I were in charge of Facebook. I've heard there is going to be a monthly fee to be on Facebook starting later in 2010. I feel fairly certain that I will still be on Facebook if I have to pay the four or six dollars a month the gurus are suggesting. I would stop Facebook if my friends left. What would the point be?

I would implement the "dislike" button. I thought I had joined a group that allowed me the opportunity to dislike without having to write "I dislike this," or "I DISlike this," depending on how strongly I felt about whatever it was.

I would maintain Facebook and get rid of the ridiculous applications so Facebook would run more smoothly. It drives me apoplectic when I write a brilliant and snarky retort to someone's post and Facebook tells me, "Oops. We're sorry; we encountered a problem. We are working on this." I think it's the "Oops" part that is so irritating to me. My gosh, this group of friends who tried to figure out a way to stay in touch after college has now created a network that is millions upon millions strong, and they are so busy adding applications that our important comments have to be repeated or rewritten or not repeated at all and our comment ends up being posted eight times.

Whenever my husband hears me typing away at the keyboard, he assumes I'm on Facebook. He'll wander into the room and nonchalantly ask me a question while peering over my shoulder. Sometimes he's right and sometimes he's not. It doesn't matter to me, though. He can read over my shoulder any time he wants. I have come to the realization that nothing on Facebook is just between friends. It's also between continents. If I wouldn't want a certain person to read my post, I don't write it.

One thing that I do is call Ken into the room and tell him to read all the wonderful things that happen because of Facebook. I'm not just showing him little bits and pieces of information, either. We have the opportunity to do really amazing things through social networks. My friends and I aren't the only ones; everyone does. So go out and clean up *your* part of the world and invite your friends. You all will be glad you did.